F. W. R. N.

MUIRHEAD LIBRARY OF PHILOSOPHY

An admirable statement of the aims of the Library of Philosophy was provided by the first editor, the late Professor J. H. Muirhead, in his description of the original programme printed in Erdmann's *History of Philosophy* under the date 1890. This was slightly modified in subsequent volumes to take the form of the following statement:

'The Muirhead Library of Philosophy was designed as a contribution to the History of Modern Philosophy under the heads: first of Different Schools of Thought – Sensationalist, Realist, Idealist, Intuitivist; secondly of different Subjects – Psychology, Ethics, Aesthetics, Political Philosophy, Theology. While much had been done in England in tracing the course of evolution in nature, history, economics, morals and religion, little had been done in tracing the development of thought on these subjects. Yet the "evolution of opinion is part of the whole evolution".

'By the co-operation of different writers in carrying out this plan it was hoped that a thoroughness and completeness of treatment, otherwise unattainable, might be secured. It was believed also that from writers mainly British and American fuller consideration of English Philosophy than it had hitherto received might be looked for. In the earlier series of books containing, among others, Bosanquet's *History of Aesthetic*, Pfleiderer's *Rational Theology since Kant*, Albee's *History of English Utilitarianism*, Bonar's *Philosophy and Political Economy*, Brett's *History of Psychology*, Ritchie's *Natural Rights*, these objects were to a large extent effected.

'In the meantime original work of a high order was being produced both in England and America by such writers as Bradley, Stout, Bertrand Russell, Baldwin, Urban, Montague, and others, and a new interest in foreign works, German, French and Italian, which had either become classical or were attracting public attention, had developed. The scope of the Library thus became extended into something more international, and it is entering on the fifth decade of its existence in the hope that it may contribute to that mutual understanding between countries which is so pressing a need of the present time.'

The need which Professor Muirhead stressed is no less pressing today, and few will deny that philosophy has much to do with enabling us to meet it, although no one, least of all Muirhead himself, would regard that as the sole, or even the main, object of philosophy. As Professor Muirhead continues to lend the distinction of his name to the Library of Philosophy it seemed not inappropriate to allow him to recall us to these aims in his own words. The emphasis on the history of thought also seemed to me very timely: and the number of important works promised for the Library in the very near future augurs well for the continued fulfilment, in this and other ways, of the expectations of the original editor.

H. D. LEWIS

MUIRHEAD LIBRARY OF PHILOSOPHY

General Editor : H. D. Lewis

Professor of History and Philosophy of Religion at the University of London

The Absolute and the Atonement by DOM ILLTYD TRETHOWAN
Absolute Value by DOM ILLTYD TRETHOWAN
Action by SIR MALCOLM KNOX
The Analysis of Mind by BERTRAND RUSSELL
Ascent to the Absolute by J. N. FINDLAY
Belief by H. H. PRICE
Brett's History of Psychology edited by R. S. PETERS
Broad's Critical Essays in Moral Philosophy edited by DAVID CHENEY
Clarity is Not Enough by H. D. LEWIS
Coleridge as Philosopher by J. H. MUIRHEAD
The Commonplace Book of G. E. Moore edited by C. LEWY
Contemporary American Philosophy edited by G. P. ADAMS and W. P. MONTAGUE
Contemporary British Philosophy first and second series edited by J. H. MUIRHEAD 2nd edition
Contemporary British Philosophy third series edited by H. D. LEWIS
Contemporary Indian Philosophy edited by RADHAKRISHNAN and J. H. MUIRHEAD 2nd edition
Contemporary Philosophy in Australia edited by ROBERT BROWN and C. D. ROLLINS
The Discipline of the Cave by J. N. FINDLAY
Doctrine and Argument in Indian Philosophy by NINIAN SMART
The Elusive Mind by H. D. LEWIS
Essays in Analysis by ALICE AMBROSE
Ethics by NICOLAI HARTMANN translated by STANTON COIT 3 vols
Ethics and Christianity by KEITH WARD
The Foundation of Metaphysics in Science by ERROL E. HARRIS
Freedom and History by H. D. LEWIS
G. E. Moore: Essays in Retrospect edited by ALICE AMBROSE and MORRIS LAZEROWITZ
The Good Will: A Study in the Coherence Theory of Goodness by H. J. PATON
Hegel: A Re-examination by J. N. FINDLAY
Hegel's Science of Logic translated by W. H. JOHNSTON and L. G. STRUTHERS 2 vols
A History of Aesthetic by B. BOSANQUET 2nd edition
A History of English Utilitarianism by E. ALBEE

MUIRHEAD LIBRARY OF PHILOSOPHY

EDITED BY H. D. LEWIS

THE VARIETIES OF BELIEF

THE VARIETIES
OF BELIEF

BY

PAUL HELM

LONDON: GEORGE ALLEN AND UNWIN LTD
NEW YORK: HUMANITIES PRESS INC

First published in 1973

© George Allen & Unwin Ltd 1973

ISBN 0 04 12107 17 4

Printed in Great Britain
in 11 point Baskerville type
by Clarke, Doble & Brendon Ltd
Plymouth

TO JUDITH

PREFACE

I am grateful to various friends and colleagues, particularly John Frame, Raymond Frey, Anthony Lloyd, Stewart Sutherland and William Young, each of whom has read either the whole or parts of this book at various stages. The errors and inadequacies that remain are, of course, my responsibility. Thanks are due, as well, to Miss Denise Matthews for her skilful and tireless typing of the script, and most of all to my wife Judith for her encouragement and patience.

Part of Chapter 8 is a revised version of a paper 'Faith, Scepticism and Experiencing-As', which first appeared in *Faith and Thought* (vol. 97, No. 3, Summer 1969), and parts of Chapter 5 are taken from a paper 'Locke on Faith and Knowledge', (*Philosophical Quarterly*, vol. 23 No. 90 1973). I wish to thank the Editors of these Journals for permission to use this material here.

PAUL HELM

Department of Philosophy
University of Liverpool

ACKNOWLEDGEMENTS

Grateful acknowledgement is made to the following for permission to quote :
The Royal Institute of Philosophy for *Talk of God* ed. G. N. A. Vesey; Routledge and Kegan Paul and Schocken Books for *The Concept of Prayer*, and *Faith and Philosophical Inquiry*, both by D. Z. Phillips; *The Human World*, the Brynmill Publishing Co. Ltd., Brynmill, Swansea for "Remarks on Frazer's *Golden Bough*" by L. Wittgenstein; Cambridge University Press for *Philosophical Theology* by F. R. Tennant, Vol. I (C) Cambridge University Press; Basil Blackwell for *On Certainty* and *Lectures and Conversations on Aesthetics, Psychology and Religious Belief* both by L. Wittgenstein; New York University Press for *The Logic of Religion* by I. M. Bochenski; S. C. M. Press and Macmillan for *Do Religious Claims Make Sense?* by S. C. Brown and *Religious Language* by I. T. Ramsey; Macmillan and Cornell University Press for *Faith and Knowledge*, by John Hick, second edition (C) 1966 Cornell University Press; Macmillan and St. Martin's Press for *Faith and the Philosophers* ed. John Hick; Oxford University Press, New York, for *Language, Persons and Belief* by Dallas M. High; Allen & Unwin and Stanford University Press for *Theology and Meaning* by R. S. Heimbeck; Westminster Press for *The Institutes of the Christian Religion* by John Calvin, Vol. XX, The Library of Christian Classics edited by John T. McNeill and translated by Ford Lewis Battles. Copyright (C) MCMLX by W. L. Jenkins.

CONTENTS

B

1

INTRODUCTION

Work in the philosophy of religion in the last thirty years has focused increasingly on the language of religion. Appeals have been made to what the religious believer says, or would say, in certain situations, and attention has been called to the allegedly logical peculiarities of 'religious language'. The argument of this book is that such approaches involve an important error in philosophical method, for they rest on the mistaken assumption that the 'religious believer' has an unmistakable identity, and that 'religious language' is a distinct, homogeneous form of language. Too often it seems that unless one happens to share the particular religious outlook of the writer, religious or theological premises are being made to yield philosophical conclusions. There is an obvious need for a less question-begging procedure, one that separates the philosophy from the religion.

One way of making this separation is to distinguish religion or theology from meta-religion or meta-theology. Two lines of argument are developed in this book for this distinction. In the first chapter it is argued that the *a priori* objections that have been made against it are not cogent, and in the second chapter that the distinction is necessary if certain confusions are to be avoided. Later it is argued that the different accounts of religious belief that are offered provide a further reason for recognizing the distinction in the philosophy of religion.

There are a number of reasons for concentrating on religious belief. For one thing, belief is a topic of general philosophical interest and importance, and this makes religious belief more tractable than, say, religious experience. Ideas about religious belief have been closely related to ideas about belief in general. Further, in view of the way in which 'the believer' has figured in recent philosophy of religion it is worth asking in what senses a man might be said to be a religious believer. The various cases or models of religious belief that will be discussed in Part II will provide us with various meta-theological possibilities. The cases are distinguished not simply for the sake of scientific convenience, as a logician might distinguish senses of 'possible', but because they have in fact had an influence on the way in which people have regarded themselves as 'believers'. The four cases to be discussed are (1) Locke and Butler, (2) John Calvin and John Owen, (3) Immanuel Kant, and (4) John Hick. Attention is given to what philosophers and theologians have to say not because either class of thinker is necessarily gifted with religious insight but because as systematizers, and sometimes influential systematizers, what they say about religious belief may fairly be taken to have influenced the account which 'believers' give of their religious belief. After setting out the various types of religious belief an attempt is made, in the final Part, to show how they affect the much-discussed issue of the meaning and understanding of religious assertions.

Because the aim of the study is to make a point about philosophical methodology no grounds are offered for preferring one analysis of religious belief to another. To insist on there being different accounts of religious belief is not to imply that there is no true account, nor that it does not matter what that account is. Nor is it to imply that by some alchemical process these various models can be made compatible, different insights into one all-embracing 'truth'.

PART I

2

INTERNAL AND EXTERNAL
QUESTIONS

This study is concerned with an examination of the meaning of a cluster of expressions involving verbs such as 'know', 'believe', 'be sure', and nouns such as 'belief' and 'unbelief' as used in religion and theology.[1] For the purpose of this examination it is irrelevant whether or not people are justified in their claims to know God, or in their denials that God can ever be an object of knowledge. What matters is how expressions occurring in religious utterances, theological controversies etc. are to be understood. Are religious beliefs like beliefs about ordinary matters of fact? Are they cognitive or regulative? It will be argued that questions like these are askable and that they are meta-theological questions. In this chapter the distinction between meta-theology and theology is made clear and defended against certain objections and misunderstandings.

I

'Meta-' enquiries are concerned with the cognitive status that an expression in a particular segment of discourse has or may have. This is sometimes said to be an enquiry into that expression's meaning. For instance, does a particular predicate have descriptive, or emotive meaning? To ask for the meaning in this way is obviously different from asking for the meaning of a particular English word or sentence. Giving the meaning of the English word 'bogus' simply involves providing lexical equivalents in English or some other natural language. Further, both these enquiries are

[1] The terms 'religion' and 'theology' are used interchangeably. This is not because they are synonymous but because there is no discernible philosophical reason at this stage for distinguishing 'religious language' from 'theological language'. For further remarks on the relation between religious language and theological language see the present and last chapters. (There is a further sense of 'religious' in which any action done for religious reasons can be said to be religious, but this usage is not adopted here.)

to be distinguished from questions about *meaningfulness*. The meaningfulness of a sentence has to do with its point or function, its place in human activities.

When logical positivists denied that religious and ethical language had a meaning they were not denying that religious and ethical sentences made sense in English or in some other natural language, nor that such sentences could be non-cognitively meaningful. Their thesis was about the cognitive status of expressions in ethics and religion, that is, it was meta-theological and meta-ethical. Because of their premiss that science is the only source of knowledge, to deny that a proposition had a place or function in scientific enquiry (that it was scientifically *meaningful*, in the sense outlined above), was equivalent to denying that it was cognitively meaningful. That is, the thesis was *both* about the meaning or cognitive status of ethical and religious language, *and* about its meaningfulness. But if the premiss that science is the only source of knowledge is denied, then the equivalence is broken : it is possible for a proposition to be cognitive though not scientifically meaningful, in the sense that it would never form part of a scientific theory. The sense in which such propositions might be said to be *known* will be discussed in Chapter 4. Possible confusion between a thesis about meaning and one about meaningfulness is helped along by an accident of English – that words such as 'meaningless' and 'nonsense' can be used to deny both meaning *and* meaningfulness.

The distinction just made between meaning and meaningfulness is an important one for this study, and it will be discussed further and employed at various points as the argument develops.

It was stated just now that 'meta-' issues concern the 'cognitive status' of the expression. But this does not help much, because 'cognitive status' is a vague notion. In his book *Theology and Meaning*[2] R. S. Heimbeck offers what he takes to be three alternative, adequate explications of this phrase, which are worth discussing for the light they throw on the nature of meta-theology. He claims, firstly, that a good test of whether or not p is cognitively meaningful is whether it would fit into the sentence frame 'I know that . . .' and make sense.[3] Secondly, a sentence is cognitively

[2] London, 1969.
[3] ibid., pp. 31–2.

significant if and only if it can be used to make a statement which is either true or false.[4] (The use of the bi-conditional is a little odd here if Heimbeck means these characterizations of cognitive significance to be alternatives, as he does,[5] but this is unimportant here.) Thirdly, a sentence is cognitively significant if it is either analytic or a factual assertion. The second characterization has fewer difficulties, but before showing this it is necessary to discuss what Heimbeck has to say about what he calls 'meta-theological scepticism'.

He says that meta-theological scepticism, for example the position of someone such as A. J. Ayer in *Language, Truth and Logic*, is like scepticism in epistemology, for example, scepticism about knowledge of other minds. According to Heimbeck someone who argues that no amount of evidence about the present will provide us with evidence about the past is a meta-sceptic about history. By contrast, a sceptic about history has doubts about the evidence of particular claims about the past, for instance the claim that Charlemagne existed. A person who argues that no amount of evidence about the physical behaviour of others is evidence for their having minds is a meta-sceptic about other minds, and so on. Such meta-sceptical claims challenge, respectively, the intelligibility of statements about the past and statements about other minds. The meta-sceptic refuses to accept any evidence as evidence.

This analogy or parallel between theology and meta-theology, and history and meta-history (for example), will not do. For one thing, the analogy ought to lead to the view that non-cognitivism in theology is expressable as 'God may exist, but nothing can ever be known about whether he does or not, and *a fortiori* nothing can be known about what God is like'. Heimbeck is stressing, in the use he makes of the example of historical scepticism, that according to the meta-historial sceptic there can be no *knowledge* about the past. But not knowing about the past is quite compatible with believing about the past, and with a variety of other epistemic attitudes such as doubting or wishing. The meta-historical sceptic refuses to accept the evidence he is given as evidence for knowledge, but it may be evidence for less ambitious claims.

[4] ibid., pp. 32–3.
[5] ibid., p. 38.

As is often said, the trouble with this sort of sceptic is that his standards are impossibly high, but impossibly high for knowledge, not for belief.

Putting this point slightly differently it is possible to say that the sceptic about other minds doubts whether it can be known that there are other minds, the sceptic about history doubts whether anything about the past can be known. But this cannot be the same as saying that statements about other minds or about the past are not cognitively significant. If it were to say this then scepticism could never be stated as a thesis, for the sceptic doubts that p, and to doubt that p ensures that p has cognitive significance. The position of someone such as Ayer in *Language, Truth and Logic* is a much stronger one than this; Ayer did not simply doubt the truth of theological statements, but challenged the very possibility of making theological statements, true or false. Meta-theological scepticism such as this is not scepticism because it denies that theological sentences are used to make informative statements about God, but because it denies that they could be used to make such statements. Whether they are in fact so used does not arise.

Part of the source of this confusion may lie in the term 'cognitive'. It can be used to characterize a proposition that may be the object of an epistemic verb such as 'believe' or 'doubt' or 'know', or it can refer to a proposition making a definite knowledge-claim. In 'I hope that Charlemagne existed' the proposition 'that Charlemagne existed' may be said to have cognitive significance, but 'I hope that Charlemagne existed' is not cognitive in the sense that it makes a knowledge-claim, for no such claim is made with these words. Positivists have denied cognitive significance to theological utterances in the sense that it is never in order to make a statement of the form 'I believe that God exists' on the grounds that 'that God exists' is unverifiable and so could never be known.

According to Heimbeck 'A sentence is cognitively significant, then, if and only if the reading of that sentence into the frame "I know . . ." makes sense'. But what is it for 'I know that p' or 'I believe that p' to make sense? According to positivism p makes sense and *a fortiori* 'I believe that p' makes sense if and only if p is verifiable by sense-experience. Does this mean that a religious person who accepts the arguments of the positivist is debarred from using the form of words 'I believe that God . . .'? Of course not. The meta-theological sceptic who is still a religious person (a 'believer' in some sense still to be discussed), can still say 'I believe that God . . .' but give the expression a different sense by, for instance, denying that 'God' denotes a being who transcends sense-experience and by adopting some form of reductionism, or by using 'believe' in a non-cognitive way. Appealing to sentence-frames in the way that Heimbeck does is nothing like rigorous enough.

The third of his characterizations, 'A sentence is cognitively significant if and only if it can be used to make either an analytic assertion or a factual assertion'[6] is open to a different objection, at least in the case of theology. This is that some would want to say both that 'God exists' is a cognitively significant sentence and that to come to believe in God's existence is not like coming to believe in the existence of an additional fact, as coming to believe in the existence of flying saucers is coming to recognize additional facts about the world. God, it is said, if he exists, is not an additional fact about the world, but he is the source of all facts. He is not a fact in our world; we are facts in his world. This is less an objection against the cognitive significance of religious utterances than a refusal to discuss religion in such terms. (There is, in addition, a general objection to the idea that it is possible to speak of 'the facts' independently of the logical grammar of a particular activity. The sort of philosophy of religion that makes this kind of point will be discussed later in the chapter; the objection is noted here.)

Heimbeck is on much stronger ground in characterizing cognitive significance in terms of truth and falsity, though it appears that he would regard an analysis of sentences such as 'God ø's' in terms of the states of mind of religious people as lacking cognitive significance, which it does not, any more than subjectivism in ethics necessarily implies non-cognitivism. If this characterization is accepted, then meta-theology will be concerned with an investigation into the kinds of truth-conditions that are applicable to theological utterances, if any. And a meta-theological study of religious belief will be concerned, among other things, with the

[6] ibid., p. 33.

truth-conditions, if any, of a range of utterances of the form 'Jones believes that God is . . .'

II

Some would say that a proper understanding of 'Jones believes that p' where 'believes' is a case of religious belief involves an investigation of the depth-grammar of religion, that is, of what it makes sense to say in religion. They would say that an analysis of religious belief is necessarily internal to the 'form of life' of religion. Just as 'I know that I am in pain' and 'I know that the Tories are in power' have the same surface-grammar but differ in their depth-grammar (this can be seen by showing, for example, that while it makes sense to doubt whether the Tories are in power it makes no sense to doubt whether or not I am in pain), so 'I believe in the Last Judgement' and 'I believe in wearing braces' have dissimilar depth-grammars which can only be brought out by exhibiting the respective 'forms of life' of each.

This position involves a denial of the distinction between theology and meta-theology as stated above. For it makes the truth-conditions of religious utterances *internal* to the form of life of religion. One result of this present study of religious belief, if it is successful, will be to show that within the Christian tradition, to look no further, very different notions of 'belief' have been operative from time to time, and that to assume that 'religious belief' has just one set of features is to beg important questions. In the remainder of this chapter the following two claims will be defended :

(*a*) That the distinction between theology and meta-theology is a valid one.

(*b*) That it is wrong and misleading exclusively to identify theology or religion with 'talk of God' or 'talk about God'.

In a review of C. B. Martin's *Religious Belief* G. E. Hughes asks 'Must one hold an orthodox meta-theology before one can be said to subscribe to an orthodox theology? Indeed, is there (could there be) an orthodox meta-theology; or are there only orthodox doctrines, not orthodox doctrines abut doctrines?'[7] This is an interesting, but a confused question. While there is a dis-

[7] *Australasian Journal of Philosophy* (1962), p. 217.

tinction between theology and meta-theology it is impossible to think of the meta-questions as being logically insulated, or in a logically different category, from the object-questions. Because, though there is a distinction between theology and meta-theology, the language of theology ('doctrine') requires a commitment to a particular meta-theology. To subscribe to a theology requires one to subscribe to a meta-theology. Unless, that is, to 'subscribe to a theology' is simply to give one's assent to a series of sentences or utterances and stoutly to resist any attempts to offer an account of them, that is, to refuse to say what one has subscribed to means. This would be to hold what amounts to a 'strict autonomist' view of religious language, in which the only sort of 'analysis' envisagable is the elucidation of the meaning of religious utterances by other religious utterances on the same level, within the same 'language game'.

To help in developing these points Carnap's distinction between internal and external questions will be employed.[8] Briefly, internal questions are questions *within* a particular conceptual framework in which a problem is raised, external questions are *about* the framework. So that the question 'Do material objects exist?', considered as an external question, is about whether there is to be a system of rules governing a concept 'material object', whereas 'Does this paper exist?', considered as an internal question, is to be answered in terms of the rules governing the use of material-object concepts. Assertions and questions within a conceptual framework will be said to constitute part of the object-language, assertions and questions about the framework the meta-language.

In the object-language of religion a religious believer can use expressions, for example, in praying or singing hymns, with the word 'God' as their subject, without thereby raising, or needing to raise, questions about the ontological implications of using this denoting word,[9] just as it is possible to use 'Pegasus' as the subject of a sentence without raising the question of the existence

[8] R. Carnap, 'Empiricism, Semantics and Ontology', in L. Linksy, ed. *Semantics and the Philosophy of Language* (1952).

[9] The discussion that follows owes a good deal to James Cornman's *Metaphysics, Reference and Language*, especially Chapter 5 'Internal and External Questions'. See also A. J. Ayer's discussion of Carnap's distinction in *Russell and Moore* (1971), pp. 182ff.

of a creature denoted by the word. The believer who subscribes to the truth of 'God exists' is not thereby committed to attaching any particular sense to the sentence. He is committed to attaching *some* sense to it, but not any particular sense. If asked what the denoting word 'God' refers to he can answer with a roughly synonymous religious phrase from the language of worship, such as 'the Lord'. It is quite possible for the believer to answer the question 'What do you mean by "God"?' by substituting other denoting expressions that are roughly equivalent in the usage of his religion. That is, he can treat the question as an internal question. The use of these denoting phrases does not commit the user to a particular view of religion such as theism, or to pantheism, or some other form of reductionism. They may, perhaps, be used most naturally by theists, but they do not *commit* the user to theism.

On the other hand, the question can be treated as an external question, as a question about the ontological status of whatever is denoted by 'God'. Does 'God' refer to 'the ground of being' (Tillich) or 'the power not ourselves that makes for righteousness' (Matthew Arnold) or 'A Spirit, infinite, eternal, and unchangeable, in his being, wisdom, power, holiness, justice, goodness, and truth' (Westminster Shorter Catechism)? This is an external question, just as much as 'Does "table" refer to a certain congeries of sensations or to a material substance?' is an external question.

But there seems nothing to stop whatever is taken as the referent of 'God' from entering and becoming a part of 'religious language'. Creeds employing notions such as substance and person, and referring to the creation of the universe by God, to miracles etc., can become part of a liturgy, confessions of faith such as the Westminster Confession of Faith can be recited or affirmed as acts of worship, their language used to make assertions in sermons and so forth. That is to say, while it is valid to draw the distinction between external and internal questions, it is misleading, (to put it no higher), to identify internal matters exclusively with first-order 'religious language' i.e. unreflective religious talk, and external matters with theories about religious language. To the question 'What does "God" refer to?' a religious believer might answer 'My Lord and Saviour' or he might say 'A being, infinite, eternal . . .' *Both* answers are examples of 'religious language', even though the first answer takes the question to be an internal question about religious usage, the other takes it to be an external question about ontological status. Further, there is nothing to say that questions about meaning, about what is meant by 'substance' for example, will not arise again. There is thus the possibility of an interpenetration between meta- and object-languages of a recurring kind, owing to the possibility of indefinitely transferring the meta-language into the object-language. That this transfer is possible in Christian theology and religion can be put down to at least two factors.

Firstly, as just noted, there is no restriction confining the use of meta-theological utterances to meta-contexts. There is nothing to stop them entering into 'religious language' and the idea that such language is *necessarily* 'first-order' seems to be just a dogma. And, connected with this point, there is nothing to stop someone claiming that when religious people are doing theology, that is, formulating and systematizing various doctrines from the data of revelation, this is a religious activity. If this is allowed, there cannot be a rigid distinction between religion and theology, and certainly not one that makes them correspond to first- and second-order languages respectively.

The extent of the interpenetration between religious language and meta-theology will depend on what view of theology is taken. If, like George Eliot's Adam Bede, formulating religious doctrine is a matter of 'finding names for your feelings' or if theological doctrines are 'accounts of religious affections set forth in speech' (Schleiermacher), then a distinction between theology and meta-theology might be sustained a bit longer that if it is thought that theology is the business of systematizing truths already revealed in unsystematic contexts, such as the Bible. For whereas there are no necessary philosophical implications in the object language if this is thought of as being composed of accounts of religious 'raw feels', there would seem to be such implications in some at least of the statements found in the Bible. If there are, then philosophical questions about the meaning of such statements, and about ontology, can be raised, and through discussion and acceptance come to be part of 'religious language'.

The second factor is that, historically, there has been a close connection between Christianity and philosophy. Christians have

felt the need either to give theoretical models to help the understanding of certain doctrines – and these models have often contained borrowed philosophical notions such as 'person' and
'substance' – or to defend accepted doctrine against philosophical
attacks or misunderstandings due to philosophical factors.

For these reasons it appears that G. E. Hughes's questions
about the compatibility or otherwise of any given meta-theology
with any given theology are misplaced. It is a mistake to think
of ontological questions, for example, or questions about the
justification of religious claims, as external questions, and so as
alien to the real business of religion and to the philosopher's
interest in religion. Differences in ontology can be religious differences. Religious questions are not simply about rules for certain
linguistic practices, they also concern ontological questions. So
that Berkeley's dictum à propos perception, to 'think with the
learned and speak with the vulgar' will not hold for religion.
Vulgar religious talk often raises learned questions, and religious
talk is often learned.

Someone might object that thinking learnedly about God is an
alien intrusion into religion. But this, to be sustained, would
have to be argued, and an appeal to the 'grammar' of religion
is not by itself going to be a strong enough argument, as will be
demonstrated later.

There is an interesting similarity between positivists such as
Rudolf Carnap and those who, like D. Z. Phillips, appeal to the
grammar of religion to validate religious language. Carnap
thought that when James Cornman calls E_2 questions, questions
the answers to which lie outside the jurisdiction of rules governing a particular operation, and which would not entail a change
in or an addition to rules governing the operation,[10] are pseudo-
questions because of his acceptance of the verification principle.
Phillips's reaction is similar : because the 'form of life' (e.g. religion) exists, the reality that it embodies in its language exists.
In his view it involves a confusion of internal and external questions to raise questions about, say, the ontological status of what
is talked about by referring to expressions in the religious form
of life in other than religious terms. For him the only permissible
external question is 'Is the language-game coherently played?',

[10] Cornman, op. cit., p. 167.

just as for Carnap the only permissible external questions are those that call for a decision, that are practical, not requiring assertions but involving changes in or additions to the rules governing certain operations.[11]

There are other similarities as well. Later positivists such as Otto Neurath and Carnap reacted against what they considered to be the metaphysical difficulties that Schlick had got himself into on the question of the relation between experience and the meaning and truth of propositions. Neurath and Carnap sought to overcome this by the introduction of the notion of a protocol statement, and a coherence theory of truth. Protocol statements then became corrigible like any other empirical sentence.[12]

Though this conventionalism was regarded by Carnap as purely syntactical, consisting of sets of formation and transformation rules, in fact this was not the case. In his use of terms such as 'experience expressions' he smuggled in a semantical component. As Ayer puts it, Carnap

'assumes that questions about the nature of immediate experience are linguistic in character. And this leads him to dismiss all the "problems of the so-called given or primitive data" as depending only upon our choice of a form of language. But this is to repeat the error of Neurath and Hempel, which we have already exposed. If the term "protocol-statement" was being used merely as a syntactical designation for certain combinations of symbols then our choice of the sentences to which we applied it would

[11] For a discussion of Carnap's attitude to external questions see Cornman, op. cit., p. 179ff. It is worth remembering at this point that in the *Tractatus* Wittgenstein rejected Russell's Theory of Types. The distinction he replaced it by, between *saying* and *showing*, Wittgenstein called 'the main point' of the *Tractatus*. (Quoted by G. E. M. Anscombe *An Introduction to Wittgenstein's Tractatus* (1959), p. 161.) It is possible to argue that the Tractarian idea of what can only be shown gets transmuted later, into the idea of various 'forms of life'. In both doctrines the distinction between meta- and object-languages is rejected. And just as, earlier, the sense of a proposition must show itself, so, later, the sense of a proposition can only be learned by reference to its 'form of life'. (Such a connection between the 'earlier' and 'later' Wittgenstein is argued for by Peter Winch, 'The Unity of Wittgenstein's Philosophy', in *Studies in the Philosophy of Wittgenstein*, ed. Winch (1969).)

[12] For a sketch of these changes see A. J. Ayer's editorial introduction to *Logical Positivism* (1959), especially Section III.

C

indeed be a matter of convention. It would involve no more reference to truth than a decision to apply the designation "basic" to all English sentences beginning with B. But this is not the sense in which Carnap is supposed to be using the term. He is using it not to mark out the form of certain statements, but rather to express the fact that they refer to what is immediately given. Accordingly, our answer to his question "What kinds of word occur in protocol-statements?" cannot depend simply upon a conventional choice of linguistic forms. It must depend upon the way in which we answer the question "What objects are the elements of given, direct experience?" And this is not a matter of language, but a matter of fact.'[13]

Further, proponents of the coherence theory of truth were faced with a problem about arbitrariness. If it is possible to have formal systems that are incompatible with each other, who is to decide between the rival merits of each?

'For any fairy tale there may be constructed a system of protocol statements by which it would be sufficiently supported; but we call the fairy tale false and the statements of empirical science true, though both comply with that formal criterion.'[14]

The only way of settling this envisaged by Carnap and Neurath was empirical. That system is accepted 'which is actually adopted by mankind, and especially by the scientists of our culture circle'.[15]

Both these points, the conventionalism and the charge of arbitrariness, are worth comparing with the problems faced by a philosopher of religion such as Phillips.

As stated earlier, Phillips has taken over the Carnapian idea that 'the reality of anything is nothing else than the possibility of its being placed in a certain system' and his views on 'the relativity of all philosophical theses in regard to language'.[16] His

[13] 'Verification and Experience', in *Logical Positivism*, ed. Ayer, pp. 237–8.

[14] C. Hempel, 'On the Logical Positivists' theory of truth', *Analysis* (January 1935), p. 56.

[15] ibid., p. 57.

[16] R. Carnap, *Philosophy and Logical Syntax* (1935), pp. 20, 78.

doctrine of language-games takes the place of Carnap's formation rules. But for Phillips, appeal to language-games is more than a syntactical matter (as, in effect, Carnap's appeal to logical syntax was), because it is coupled with an epistemology that rests on the denial of a private language. Language is necessarily public because 'rule-following'. This ensures that Phillips's 'formation rules', the logical grammar in accordance with which language-games are played, have content, but it raises the spectre of arbitrariness.

But is this fair? Is it not rather that the charge of arbitrariness is *avoided* by appeal to the language-game of religion? There is this appeal, but it does not remove the arbitrariness. For who says which of the manifold utterances of religion is 'grammatical'? This question is especially acute for someone who wishes, as Phillips does, to distinguish between a believer's faith and the often 'confused accounts' of his beliefs.[17] Who is to say, on philosophical grounds, what is light and what is darkness? To say 'The language-game is played!' does not settle, for instance, the ontological status of 'God' in the religious language-game. Given, for the sake of the argument, that 'what the believer says' provides the philosopher of religion with well-formed sentences, who decides what the transformation rules are to be? Who decides what can legitimately be inferred from the believer's expressions of belief?

Phillips has two answers to these questions. The first is to acknowledge that there are many religions and theologies, and that the question about the ontological status of the concept of God is theological, one to be settled within religion. Such theological differences are differences about what it makes sense to say in religion.[18] Secondly, Phillips argues that it is the function of philosophy, in religion as elsewhere, to show which of the many accounts that are given of religion are confused. Philosophy does not show the activities and beliefs of religion to be confused – how could it? Rather, it shows certain accounts of religion to be confused, and it does this by appealing to 'grammar'.

These two points are sufficient to make it perfectly clear that for Phillips religious language is not just a set of symbols oper-

---

[17] e.g. D. Z. Phillips, *Death and Immortality* (1970), pp. 69–70.
[18] D. Z. Phillips ed., *Faith and Philosophical Enquiry* (1970), p. 128.

able according to certain rules, and otherwise pointless. Not to
see this is, as Phillips puts it, to confuse 'the conditions of intelligibility with the content of what is said'.[19]

However, certain matters are still not clear. Suppose some say
that there is a trinity of persons in the Godhead, while others
deny this. On Phillips's view this is an example of a theological
disagreement over which philosophy has no say. Some religious
people, like the Sadduccees, say that there is no survival after
death, while others say that there is a life after death. This
difference is philosophical, not theological, according to Phillips.
For if we engage in intellectual clarification of the issue, we
shall see that hopes of life after death are meaningless. They
cannot stand up to philosophical scrutiny. The puzzle is why
certain religious claims are exempt from scrutiny, while others
are not. If the history of Western philosophy has shown anything,
it has shown that theological doctrines such as creation, divine
foreknowledge, human responsibility, eternity and immortality
raise philosophical questions.

III

In a recent discussion *Do Religious Claims Make Sense?*[20] S. C.
Brown makes a distinction between internal and external questions, and also between what he calls grammatical and meta-
grammatical claims in religion. These distinctions look like the
distinction between theology and meta-theology just made, but
there are significant differences. Following Wittgenstein's suggestions about regarding theology as grammar Brown suggests that
the articles of faith of a religion constitute its grammar.[21]
Theology has the task of systematizing what it makes sense to
say in a religion. If, for example, one article of faith says 'no
true believer can ever be lost' the 'can' here is grammatical. It is
not an empirical statement such as 'no sheep can get out of this
field'. It lays down what, for that religion, it *means* to be a believer. A 'believer' who apostatizes is to be thought of as never

[19] ibid., pp. 126, 130.
[20] London, 1969.
[21] Brown, op. cit., p. 147. Wittgenstein's remark in *Philosophical Investigations* (Second Edition, 1958), para. 373. ('Grammar tells what kind of an
object anything is. Theology as grammar'.)

having been a believer. Further, within a religion there are
matter-of-fact claims: 'Whether or not a man is a "saint",
whether or not a given course of action is "God's will" for a
given man, these are, within the language of the Christian religion, *questions of fact*'.[22]. It was shown in the last section that
D. Z. Phillips has a similar way of putting this point, namely
that the grammar of a religion signifies what is real, including
the reality of God. It says what sort of reality God has.[23] To
adopt the language of religion is to adopt a further sense of
reality, just as to adopt a material object-language is to sanction
talk of the reality of the external world. It makes sense to ask
about the existence of tables and chairs only *within* the material
object-language, and it only makes sense to ask about the existence of God within the religious language-game.

Brown argues that, if the question 'Does God exist?' is asked
as a question external to the grammar of religion, it is a question
about what is presupposed by the acceptance of certain grammatical claims (it is 'meta-grammatical'), whereas if it is raised
as an internal question it asks whether a non-theistic grammar
of religion is possible. Neither as an external question nor as an
internal question is the existence of God a matter of fact. It is
worth noticing at once that Brown takes it for granted, in these
remarks, that the question 'Does God exist?' has a particular
sense; that, for example, to answer the question in the negative
is to deny theism, and not to deny pantheism or some other view.

When Brown talks of grammatical remarks about God, for
instance, he means what it makes sense to say that God can
do or undergo. For example, 'Can God be mocked?' is a grammatical question. But there is a whole range of questions about
the role of 'God' as a denoting expression which talk of the
grammar of 'God' in this way does not cover, but which are
nevertheless questions about the meaning of religious language.
They are not what Brown calls 'meta-grammatical', but concern
the ontological status of God.

So that besides Brown's distinction between grammatical and
meta-grammatical questions there is need for the further distinc-

---

[22] ibid., p. 148.
[23] D. Z. Phillips, 'Faith, Scepticism and Religious Understanding', in D.
Z. Phillips ed., *Religion and Understanding* (1967), p. 67.

tion between those questions that concern the sense of denoting
words and phrases in religious discourse (e.g. 'God' refers to 'an
infinite, eternal spirit'), and those questions that concern what it
makes sense to say in religious activities such as worship (e.g.
'God will not forsake his people'). This reinforces the point made
earlier, that though in religion and theology the distinction between object- and meta-questions is real enough it cannot be
drawn in terms of what the believer says as against what the
believer says about what he says. For these are not two logically
separate activities.

These points can perhaps be better made by referring to some
of Brown's remarks on J. A. T. Robinson's anti-theistic views.
These views can, according to Brown, be taken to be meta-
grammatical. That is, they can be taken as raising the question
of the possibility of what a non-theistic language of religion might
be like.[24] Just as Berkeley denied material substance to be necessary for a satisfactory account of perception so Robinson, according to Brown, denies that theism is necessary for religion. Just
as for Berkeley the existence of the external world consisted in
having a stable, coherent perception of sensations, so for Robinson the existence of God is identical not with the existence of a
transcendent being (traditional theism) but with 'ultimate reality'.
This does not mean that Robinson denies that God (in some
sense of 'God') exists, any more than Berkeley denies that the
external world (in some sense of 'external world') exists. According to Robinson 'God' denotes 'ultimate reality' just as for
Berkeley 'external world' denotes a certain class of sensations.

Brown presents Berkeley as arguing that the existence of God
is required by the language of perception, and claims that it might
be possible in a parallel way to show that the existence of God
is necessary for the language and practice of religion.[25] To argue
this, Brown says, is analogous to Locke, who argued that material
substance is necessary for the language of perception. And, in
Brown's view, Robinson plays Berkeley to *this* Locke.[26] But this

[24] They might also be taken as what Cornman calls E_1 questions, questions
about the convenience, economy, etc., of certain religious expressions. If
taken in this way, Robinson is not raising ontological questions at all, but
simply proposing changes in terminology for pragmatic religious gains.

[25] Brown, op. cit., p. 156.

[26] ibid., p. 157.

is not so. For it it is no part of Robinson's claim to deny that the existence of God is necessary for religion. Robinson denies the God of theism but not God *in some sense of the word*. Berkeley denies material substance, but not the external world nor the 'talk of the vulgar'. And because Robinson does not deny that it is necessary for religion that God exists, it is hard to see how he can be said to be making a meta-grammatical point, denying that the existence of God is a necessary presupposition for religion.

For all its apparent popularity, this comparison between Robinson and theism, and Berkeley and Locke, might not be very apt. For they both accepted 'ordinary talk' about the external world, for example. So that if the argument is in terms of what they would have said in the object-language then nothing changes : they would both have said the same. But Robinson and his opponents would not both say the same. At least, though on occasion they might use the same words on other occasions they clearly would not. Robinson, for example, would not use the statements of the Westminster Shorter Catechism to expound his idea of God.[27]

Anyone who worships God is committed to the existence of

---

[27] A nice, historically important, example of unwillingness to use certain concepts to express religious belief is the following: 'The Arians, those eminent masters of pretence and dissimulation, did not reject any one form of speech, which the Catholics had adopted and used, either out of Scripture or from tradition, with the sole exception of the word ὁμοούσιος; as being a word of which the precision and exactness precluded all attempt at equivocation. When they were asked, whether they acknowledged that the Son was begotten of the Father Himself? they used to assent, understanding, as is plain, the Son to be of God in such sense as all creatures are of God, that is, have the beginning of their existence from him. When the Catholics enquired of them, whether they confessed that the Son of God was God, they forthwith answered, "Most certainly". Nay more, they used of their own accord openly to declare that the Son of God is true God. But in what sense? Forsooth being *made* true God, He is true God; that is, He is true God who was truly *made* God. Lastly, when they were charged by the Catholics with asserting that the Son of God is a creature, they would repel the charge, not without some indignation, with the secret reservation of its being in this sense, that the Son of God is not *such* a creature as all other creatures are, – they being created by God *mediately* through the Son, not immediately as the Son himself. The word ὁμοούσιος, "of one substance", was the only expression which they could not in any way reconcile with their heresy.' Bull, *Defensio Fidei Nicenae* (1685). Quoted in W. G. T. Shedd, *History of Christian Doctrine* (1872), vol. 1, p. 312.

God just as anyone who washes the dishes is committed to the external world. The crucial question concerns the sense of this commitment. Robinson is not an atheistic thelogian, but he is trying to give a different *sense* to the language of theism and to reject certain traditional classic interpretations.

It may be that terminological difficulties are to blame for a certain amount of the confusion here : 'atheism' can be taken to be the denial of classical theism, or more generally as the denial of the existence of God in some sense or other. In the former sense of the term Robinson is an atheist, but not in the latter sense. 'Non-theistic theology' and 'atheist theology' are not equivalent expressions. So that Robinson is not denying the necessary existence of God, nor that *much* (but not all) of the traditional language about God may have a use (though on this see footnote 24 above), but he is trying to give this talk a different sense.

It would not be accurate to say that Brown completely misses this point. He sees that what Robinson is doing is

're-interpreting what it is theology is about. For, in *some* sense, an atheistic theology is obviously a contradiction in terms. But not in *any* sense. For the adequacy of the accepted concept of "theos" may itself be questioned. The contradiction may thus be retained, but placed elsewhere.'[28]

But he makes this point only at the expense of confusing his use of the (for him) crucial term 'grammatical'. For Robinson's point here is not meta-grammatical, not about what is presupposed by acceptance of certain grammatical claims – God is presupposed – but one about the sense of denoting expressions used in the religious language of Christianity.

The failure to see this, and the general neglect of questions about the sense to be given to denoting expressions in religious language, is due, probably, to Brown's conception of religion as a language, and to the view that he holds in common with Phillips, that the distinction between what is real and unreal in religion is to be found within the language itself.[29] If 'the notion of "correspondence with reality" cannot be used to give *content* to language, for *its* content needs to be specified by reference to

[28] Brown, op. cit., p. 157.
[29] ibid., p. 49.

the field of discourse into which it enters',[30] then it is clear that within such a language the question of reductionism cannot be raised.

It is unsatisfactory simply to say that the language-game of religion defines the reality of God, for this prevents questions about, for example, religious belief, about possible different grounds that believers have for their beliefs, and about how what is believed is to be understood. The temptation is to say 'The sort of reality defines the sort of belief; hence religious belief is of *this* kind or it is superstitious or impossible to understand'. A philosopher who takes this view of religious language as being strictly autonomous precludes himself from investigating different notions of belief occurring in religion because for him the object of belief is non-contingently connected with the belief, and with the affective and other attitudes that go with it, such as praise and thanksgiving, fear and hope. These criticisms, with particular reference to religious belief, are developed in the next chapter.

Brown's distinction between theology as grammar and meta-grammatical issues blurs the issues that reductionism raises in religion and theology because the reductionist, (in at least one of the senses of 'reductionism' to be discussed below), and the non-reductionist may both adhere in good faith to the same articles of faith; that is, in Brown's terms, their religious grammars might be the same, yet their ontologies different.

It is just possible that, by regarding articles of faith as spelling out the grammar of religion, Brown means that, if someone gives the terms in the articles of faith a different sense, this entails a difference in grammar. In this case particular definitions would be crucial to the grammaticalness of an expression, and a proposal to redefine God, in the manner of J. A. T. Robinson, would be a grammatical proposal. This may be what Brown means. On the other hand the impression that he gives in most of his discussion is that the only issue between Robinson and traditional theism is *meta*-grammatical, concerned with whether or not the existence of the God of classical theism is necessary to the language of the Christian religion, and that Robinson and his opponents share the same articles of faith.

[30] ibid., p. 49.

IV

In the previous section it was claimed that, under circumstances where the meaning of an expression can be given independently of ontology, reductionism is not statable as an issue. This requires a certain amount of qualification. It is notorious that what looks like reductionism from one philosophical standpoint looks innocuous enough from another. This is because reductionism is relative to ontology. The reductionist denies the meaningfulness of part of the non-reductionist's ontology, and so has no philosophical conscience on the matter. If the notion of material substance is meaningless, how can it be reductionist to deny substance? The anti-reductionist, with his different philosophical account of the disputed entities, regards his opponent as wishing to de-populate the universe.

From the standpoint of religious discourse, the remarks of Brown and Phillips are not reductionist. Ontologically speaking, neither wishes to get rid of anything. That is, there is a resistance to the sort of reductionism advanced by R. B. Braithwaite in *An Empiricist's View of the Nature of Religious Belief* in which statements about God are said to be nothing but statements about moral attitudes. Nor is Phillips committed to reductionism in the sense that he wishes to do without references to history in religious language, to analyse them away. He is quite prepared to allow that religious language derives nourishment from history, and that the connection between religious language and history is a non-contingent one.

Where a Phillips-type position is reductionist is in its proposal to correct or reform religious language according to the supposed 'grammar' of religion. This reductionism is a proposal within religion, and amounts to the provision of a new model for the understanding of, for example, divine transcendence, given the (for Phillips) unacceptable model of classical theism. The reductionist character of this programme shows most clearly in his remarks about immortality and the Last Judgement.[31]

---

[31] On the sense in which Phillips's views may be said to be reductionist, see Alan Brunton, 'A model for the religious philosophy of D. Z. Phillips', *Analysis*, vol. 31, No. 2 (Dec. 1970). Phillips may say that he is restoring an old model of transcendence, not offering a new one.

It may help to set out the different senses in which it is possible to speak of reductionism in religion. There are three, possibly four, kinds of 'reductionist' thesis :

(a) A thesis involving the analysis of reference to historical events in a set of propositions into non-historical ones, into, for example, moral predicates. Kant may be regarded as a reductionist in this sense in distinguishing as he does between 'ecclesiastical' and 'pure religious' faith. Pure religious faith makes no necessary reference to contingent events, whereas ecclesiastical faith does.

(b) A thesis analysing transcendent terms into immanent terms. Such an analysis does not *necessarily* involve any denial of the transcendent character of God, but offers a certain model as an elucidation of the transcendence of God, and even perhaps as a proof of it, because for general epistemological reasons no other model is available. Kant would again provide an example of this in his 'moral reductionism', and his moral proof of the existence of God. This kind of reductionism is neither entailed by, nor entails, reductionism of the first kind. Phillips's account of prayer and immortality would be reductionist in this sense.

(c) A thesis analysing transcendent terms into immanent terms without remainder. This is not simply to offer a *model* of transcendence, (say, in moral terms, as Kant does), but to claim in effect, that the transcendent-sounding language of religion means nothing over and above certain immanent states of affairs. Braithwaite and Hegel would be examples of two (very different) reductionists in this sense.

(d) A possible fourth case would be the analysis of religious language into non-religious. This is mentioned in an article by J. C. Thornton[32] but it is not clear what he has in mind until the very fuzzy notion of religious language can be made clear. If his view is not already covered by one of the above, he may be referring to currently-popular attempts to construct 'secular' theologies. But it is not clear that, even if such theologies were constructible, this would be a case of analysis into non-religious language. If they catch on, might not the secular theologies of today be the sacred theologies of tomorrow ?

In his otherwise helpful discussion of reductionist theologies

[32] 'Religious Belief and Reductionism', *Sophia*, vol. 5, No. 3, October 1966.

in *Sense, Nonsense and Christianity*[33] Hugo Meynell does not make these different senses of 'reduction' clear. It is not simply the case, as he suggests, that there are different reductionist strategies employing different categories on the right-hand side of the equation; it is also the case that the ideas of what it is to reduce the left-hand side to the right-hand side differ. To treat Hegel and Kant as two species of the same genus, as Meynell does, is therefore misleading.

V

The discussion of religious belief that we are about to embark on is meta-theological in character, in the sense discussed and accepted in Section II of this chapter. That is, the focus will be on questions about the truth conditions of various kinds of religious belief. Because the 'strict autonomist' view of religious language is rejected attention will be paid in this study to reductionist as well as non-reductionist theologies, for they provide a different set of answers to the question of what kinds of proposition someone who is said to be a religious believer might be said to believe in. When a Kantian says 'I believe in God' he means something different from a Reformed theologian such as John Owen, and his belief has different practical implications from those of Owen. One of the purposes of looking at various models of religious belief is to bring out such implications, and the connection they have, or may have, with the much-discussed issue of verification and falsification in religion. The account of religious belief given by those who take a strict autonomist view of religious language will be examined along with other views. But when philosophers refer to 'the believer' and to what the believer says or might say, in the hope of cutting off certain objections to religious belief as such, and to rival accounts of religious belief, their view can be shown to be *a priori* and to beg just those questions that are at issue. 'What the believer says' is the beginning of the philosophy of religion, or one segment of it; it does not constitute an end-all argument. This claim will be argued further in the next chapter.

[33] London, 1964, Ch. 4.

3

RELIGIOUS LANGUAGE–SOME
CONTEMPORARY APPROACHES

It was argued in the last chapter that the distinction between theology and meta-theology is valid and important, and that it cannot be avoided by what was called the 'strict-autonomy appeal', by an appeal to the 'grammar' of religious language.[1] Further, the distinction between theology and meta-theology does not correspond in any simple way to the distinction between what it makes sense to say 'in religion' and the possibility of religion as a 'form of life'. There is not simply one meta-question, the question of whether religion is possible or not, but many meta-questions, about the objects of religious belief and the epistemological status of religious beliefs, for example. The final point made was that, granted the theology meta-theology distinction, it is a mistake to think of theology or religion as exclusively identical with 'religious language' and meta-theology as something else, because meta-theological questions can be raised or can occur in 'religious language'.

In the present chapter it will be argued that certain contemporary analyses of 'religious language' fail *either* because they ignore the theology meta-theology distinction and consider an appeal to 'what the believer says' to be straightforward and uncontroversial, *or* because they regard 'religious language' as *sui generis* ('logically odd') and religious belief and disbelief to be *sui generis* as well.

[1] 'Strict autonomy' is contrasted with 'weak autonomy'. By 'weak autonomy' is meant the view that religious discourse has characteristically different aims from, say, discourse in physics in that it serves different needs or interests, while leaving open the question of how sense and nonsense, and truth and falsity are to be determined in religion. It is not clear whether this 'weak autonomist' view implies that there is a distinctive 'logic' of religious language.

I

In *The Concept of Prayer*[2] D. Z. Phillips says that according
to Wittgenstein 'if a philosopher wants to give an account of religion, he must pay attention to what religious believers do and
say'.[3] By 'what religious believers say' is not meant what religious
believers say about their religious beliefs and activities, such as
prayer. The 'appeal to ordinary language' is not to be equated
with collecting the views of religious people in a straightforward
empirical way, as the views of people on the Common Market
might be collected, by a questionnaire, for example. Nor is
such an appeal to be conducted on the assumption, which Phillips finds in contemporary philosophers such as Flew and Hep-
burn, that when a religious person is using a term he is using it
literally. Nor, by extension, would Phillips say that the 'appeal'
can be made by consulting standard documents such as confessions of faith and theological treatises. All these appeals are cases
of writers mistaking talk *about* religion with the talk of someone
engaged in religion. It will be apparent from the discussion in
the last chapter that this distinction between talk about religion
and talk when engaged in religion is an unfruitful one unless a
sharp distinction can in fact be made between the activity of
religion and what is said about it. It is the argument of the
first part of the present chapter that no non-arbitrary distinction
of this kind can be made. 'Study the ritual not the belief' might
be a useful slogan in anthropology but it cannot be useful in
the philosophy of religion, not even when the rituals are the
linguistic rituals of prayer or preaching. A possible retort to this –
that to study the linguistic ritual is to study the belief – is not
obviously true. Part of the argument that follows is directed to
this retort as well.

Phillips's claim is that the appeal ought to be not to what believers say *about* their religious activities, but what they say *in*
them. Only in this way does religion disclose its sense. One implication of this appeal is that religious believers all do something
typical, and that what they do is readily identifiable as religious.

[2] London, 1965.
[3] ibid., p. 1.

Phillips is not saying that there are not many religions, but that what makes an activity or utterance religious is its connection with a certain 'form of life'.

One thing that is interesting about philosophical claims of this sort is what their attitude is to possible counter-examples. Phillips recognizes the enormous variety of activities that go under the name of prayer.

'If one does try to give an account of prayer as a religious practice, one soon realizes that this is a difficult undertaking. To begin with, one is confronted by the diversity of the subject, one discovers that people have very different ideas about prayer. Inevitably one's own ideas of prayer impose themselves on one's investigation, singling out those prayers towards which one is sympathetic from those with which one feels little sympathy or no sympathy at all.'[4]

Faced with this mass of data the investigator can only follow his own interests. But Phillips's remarks suggest that it is not simply the case that in order to limit the field he has focused on a certain range of cases. For of certain prayers he says 'I do not say that they are not prayers (who is a philosopher to say that?), but simply that I do not understand what is involved in them'.[5] That is, the selection of cases is not methodological but is due to the fact that Phillips does not understand such prayers. On the one hand he takes the view that the criteria of meaningfulness are to be found *within* religion, on the other hand that certain prayers are incomprehensible to him. Does this mean that the prayers that are not understood are not prayers? If there are prayers that he does not understand, how can he be in a position to identify mistakes or confusion in religion? If there are words or sentences in a natural language that a person does not

---

[4] ibid., p. 7.

[5] ibid., p. 8. In order to grasp this point it is necessary to bear in mind the distinction made previously between the *meaning* and the *meaningfulness* of a sentence. Phillips is not saying that when certain prayers are incomprehensible to him he does not understand the English sentences in which the prayers are made, but that he does not see the religious point of praying such prayers. 'Understanding' is thus connected with the meaningfulness of the *activity* of praying, not with the meaning of sentences that find their way into prayers. This distinction will be discussed more fully in the final chapter.

understand, how can that person say that those words or sentences are being misunderstood by others?

The example that Phillips gives of a confusion here – regarding prayer as being causally efficacious – is not very helpful. Requests are not necessarily to be understood as causally efficacious in the way that the right coin is causally efficacious in a launderette. For prayers are *requests*, or at least some of them are, and requests are logically different from mechanistic causes, no matter to whom the requests are made. But because x is not mechanistically efficacious it does not follow that x is not causal and that x may not be efficacious under certain conditions. Because prayers are not mechanistic causes it does not follow that they are not necessary conditions for the production of certain effects under certain conditions, if, for example, what is requested is in accordance with God's will.

Presumably if Phillips did come to understand petitionary prayers, then his idea of what was meaningful in religion would be extended. That is, he must allow that he *could* come to understand these prayers otherwise he would be wrong to identify them as prayers, and not as 'prayers' in the first place.

Further, he claims that as a result of philosophical investigation into religion, which he likens to the cure of an illness, a person can possess an understanding that he did not have before. As a result of this growth in insight he might come to see that the religion of certain believers was shallow, or even that it was not a religion at all.[6]

So there are at least thre possibilities – that a prayer is intelligible and religiously adequate, or that it is intelligible but religiously shallow, or that it is unintelligible but still a prayer. On the one hand Phillips, following some remarks of Wittgenstein, says that the criteria of religion are internal to religion and rejects the philosopher's role as being that of tidying up religion.[7] On the other hand he wants to say that certain *prima facie* religious activities such as prayers are not intelligible as prayers, on the basis of the fact that they are unintelligible when measured against criteria that are derived from religion alone. What this suggests is that Phillips is working with a substantive

[6] ibid., pp. 10–11.
[7] ibid., p. 11.

view of religion which provides the rules of the 'grammar' of religion. This must be borne in mind when he appeals to what the believer says; it is less to what the believer says than to what he says *after* this has been tidied up by appeal to the depth-grammar of religion.

An attempt will now be made to make good this charge by making some remarks about what Phillips says about prayer and hope. Writing of religious hope, and the contrast he borrows from Simone Weil between natural and supernatural religion, Phillips says 'The religious alternative to such despair is hope. But the believer's hope is not hope *for* anything, moral improvement, for example, since he has already recognized that there is no hope of that. It is simply hope, hope in the sense of the ability to live with himself.'[8] There are two points here; the first is whether sense can be made of a hope that has nothing for its object, but this matter will not be discussed further here. The second point, given that it does make sense, is whether it is true of all religious hopes that they are not hopes for any*thing*.

A natural reaction to this claim is that what Phillips says may at best be true of some, but not of all religious hopes. Take some expressions of hope from the New Testament.

'For if the dead rise not, then is not Christ raised : and if Christ be not raised, your faith is vain; ye are yet in your sins. Then they also which are fallen asleep in Christ are perished. If in this life only we have hope in Christ, we are of all men most miserable.'[9]

It is not obvious that this is not a case of religious hope, and hope for a particular state of affairs. To sustain Phillips's position it must be argued that these are not religious hopes, or if they are religious hopes, it must be argued that they are not hopes *for* anything. Phillips's account of religious hope amounts either to a stipulation which one is free to reject, or to an analysis which as it stands is inadequate. What would be required to make such an analysis adequate is the demonstration that certain reductionist theses were necessary if traditional expressions of Christian hope were to be understood correctly. But Phillips is prevented

[8] ibid., p. 67.
[9] *I Corinthians* 15 : 16–19.

D

from arguments of this sort by his refusal to distinguish between religion and theology, and meta-religion and meta-theology.

A consideration of Phillips's distinction between natural and supernatural religion shows why religious hope is not hope for anything. The distinction is between a conception of God whose nature depends 'on one's fortunes in this life', on how things turn out for one, good or ill, and one whose nature is independent of consequences.

'No matter how varied our moral opinions might be, we do know what would count against calling such a God "good" in many instances. If our possessions were plundered, our servants killed, the house containing our children destroyed, the condemnation of most of us would be immediate if it could be shown that a God on whom we were causally dependent were responsible.'[10]

(This passage is crucial not only for understanding what Phillips says about hope, but for the position he takes on, for example, falsification and the problem of evil.) Such a God would be 'natural'. But according to Phillips, Job did not regard God in these terms; he depended on a supernatural God, for his relationship to God did not depend on how things went. In his trust or hope in God Job did not trust or hope *for* anything. 'Whatever Job meant by asserting the goodness of God, it was not that good things would happen to him.'[11]

The reason that Phillips argues in this way is that in his view it would be immoral and (hence?) irreligious to understand religious activities as in any sense teleological, as having any goal that is specifiable independently of the activity itself. One assumption that operates here is the idea that there is no position between (in ethical terms) deontology and egoism. Since Phillips does not want to think of religion as a method of self-gratification he thinks of it in completely 'deontological' terms. It could be shown that the contrast that runs throughout his study between prayer as confession, thanksgiving and contemplation on the one hand, and as a way of getting one's own way on the other is overdrawn and artificial. But this is not so much the issue here

[10] Phillips, op. cit., p. 98.
[11] ibid., p. 98.

as the fact that the account of religion, of religious hope in this case, is coloured by certain *a priori* notions about the connection between religion and morality. For this reason Phillips is liable to call petitionary prayers confused or shallow and to reject them on the grounds that they are 'ungrammatical'. It would be possible to dwell on other features of Phillips's treatment of religion that are equally *a priori* in character, but the point has perhaps been made. It is not being suggested that Phillips's view of religion is not a possible one. But his appeal to the 'grammar' of religion is based on the assumption, not borne out by evidence, that all coherent religions share a particular grammar, and that others can be shown to be confused or shallow by appeal to 'grammar'. But the 'grammatical' points that Phillips makes about hope, or about a religiously adequate conception of God, or about the silence of God (for example) rest on an *a priori* view of what religious utterances and activities must be like.[12]

II

In *The Logic of Religion*[13] I. M. Bochenski argues that the subject matter of the logic of religion is the actual discourse of religious communities. But this requires, or seems to require, a considerable amount of empirical data before firm conclusions can be made. Bochenski believes it possible to get around this problem by simply taking 'into consideration some obvious and universally known features of RD (religious discourse) and of the current behaviour of the believers'.[14]

So in considering the claim that some parts of the religious discourse of every religion are intended by their users to express and assert propositions Bochenski proposes the following procedure:

'First, we ask a believer of *r* if he believes a sentence P, which is part of the RD of *r*. He, of course, will say that he does. Then we

---

[12] In *Death and Immortality* (1970), Phillips allows that it is possible to have different 'pictures of immortality' from which different individuals 'derive sustenance' (p. 78). This seems to be a modification of the thesis argued in *The Concept of Prayer*.

[13] New York, 1965.

[14] ibid., p. 14.

ask him if he thinks that P is true. It seems that there can be no doubt about the answer : the believer will always answer that he does, that he thinks P to be true. But a formula can be true only if it means a proposition. Therefore, the believers think that some parts of RD express propositions.'[15]

Two points about this. The first is that it is a questionable assumption that believers would react to the questions put to them in this predictable way. Second, even if they did re-act as Bochenski claims, the questions put to them are clearly extremely unclear in a religious context, e.g. the question whether the believer thinks that the proposition he believes is true. How is the investigator to know that 'true' is not being used in some religiously eccentric way? 'True' because the proposition, as Cole-ridge put it, 'finds' me?

Bochenski's stress on the need for empirical data, together with the manifest lack of it, leads him to take short cuts on occasion in the development of his argument. Discussing what he calls the 'trust' theory of religion, and whether believers are in 'constant and universal direct communication' with a Reveal-ing Agency, he says :

'This question could only be answered if we had enough empiri-cal studies concerning the mass of believers. We do not possess such studies and cannot, therefore, have any scientific certainty as to this point.

'This author's personal opinion is that the theory is wrong on empirical grounds. It seems to him that there is no such continuous Revelation to the mass of believers but that they are "living in the darkness of faith".'[16]

The point about this personal opinion of Bochenski's is that it ought not to provide a premiss for a philosophical argument about religion. Nor ought a philosopher of religion to think that his work is inhibited in the absence of such data. He has at least two roles to play; one is to examine the notions that he finds in religion and theology, in Scripture, creeds and confessions, to discover what these concepts mean, their metaphysical implica-

[15] ibid., pp. 41–2.
[16] ibid., pp. 138–9.

tions and so forth. The other role that he has is to develop various models of religious notions. Neither of these roles requires a mass of empirical data, for the philosopher is concerned with logical, not empirical possibilities. The alternative to this is to wait for the data. But then the philosopher will simply be doing sociology disguised as an examination into the logic of religion, and will be basing his account of the concepts of religious belief on the behaviour of some group or groups of religious people.

A philosopher of religion is concerned with the meaning and coherence of religious claims, and not with empirical data concerning the actual incidence of religious belief. To discard an account of religious belief on empirical evidence, because the mass of believers do not use 'believe' in this way, is not a permissible move for a philosopher of religion to make, although if it is discovered that as a matter of fact no one ever uses words in the way in which a particular analysis of them claims they must be used this will be, to say the least, a *prima facie* case against such an analysis.

III

In *Religious Language*[17] I. T. Ramsey maintains that religious language has a distinctive logic, or is logically 'odd'. He writes, for example :

' "Did the Resurrection occur?" has *not* the same logic as 'Did the empty tomb occur?" if for no other reason than that the second can be asserted while the first is denied, and the second might even be, and by some has been, denied while the first has been asserted.'[18]

That is, for many people 'There was an empty tomb' is a necessary but not sufficient condition of 'There was a Resurrection', while for others it is neither necessary nor sufficient. For some 'There is a million employed' is a necessary but not a sufficient condition for 'There is a slump', while for others it is neither a necessary nor sufficient condition. But does this show that 'un-

---

[17] London, 1957.
[18] ibid., p. 127.

employment' has a different *logic* from 'slump'? To say that something has a different logic from something else suggests that the laws of logic are different in each case; that in one case the law of identity does not hold, perhaps, or that a proposition can have another value than 'true' or 'false'. What Ramsey's example (quoted above) suggests is that by 'different logic' he means nothing like this, but 'different truth-conditions'. But then why is this a peculiarity of religious language? One of the factors that makes a concept differ from another concept in *any* language is possessing different truth-conditions.

A reply to this might be that what is distinctive about religious language is that, for example, it refers to events for which there are truth-conditions that are not straightforwardly empirical. 'God' denotes a non-material agent, and if an event is the direct act of God, then some of its truth-conditions will be non-material, though the grounds which lead men to believe that an event was an act of God would be empirical: perhaps the occurrence of certain analogies between the event and a human action, coherence of the event with certain expectations derived from revelation, voices, visions etc.[19] Unless Ramsey is going to say that such empirical grounds are not necessary for believing that a miracle, and not just an ordinary event, occurred, then he must say that there are truth-conditions satisfied by the miracle that are not satisfied by the ordinary event, and that the grounds for believing that an event was a resurrection rather than merely the emptying of a tomb are empirical.

The difficulty with this as an account of Ramsey's views is that it covers only cases of miracles or alleged miracles, whereas Ramsey wishes to say that 'logical oddity' is a general feature of religious language. As a general feature of religious language the point may be that predicates are not used univocally of 'God' and 'man'. But this is the familiar, perennial issue of predication in religion and theology which does not raise any peculiarly logical issues, except that, if it is the case that there is some analogical relation between a word predicated of men and of God, it will have different logical implications in each case.

A second thing that Ramsey may mean by 'logical oddity' is

---

[19] For an interesting attempt to set out such conditions see Richard Swinburne, *The Concept of Miracle* (1970).

the familiar philosophical point that 'grammar is no guide to logic'. In a passage that occurs a little earlier than the one quoted above he writes:

'Suppose we begin by asking the question which many others have asked: "Did the Resurrection occur?" It sounds a very simple, straightforward, question, like; "Did Queen Anne's death occur?" But a moment's reflection makes it plain that, and not for the first time, grammatical similarities may be deceptive.'[20]

But they will only be deceptive if, for example, it is said that the Resurrection does not refer to an event. If it does refer to an event then it is hardly deceptive to ask of it, as of any putative event, whether it occurred or not. What will have to be done to find out whether it occurred or not is a different matter, but this epistemological point is not sufficient to count the Resurrection as logically odd. Ramsey may mean that the question 'Did the Resurrection occur?' is deceptive because the Resurrection was not even a putative event. But there is no evidence to suggest that Ramsey himself thinks this and hence no reason to think that by 'logically odd' he means, in the manner of Feuerbach, that a sentence about the Resurrection is in fact a statement about the sincere utterer of the sentence. Such anthropological reduction of theological language seems to be quite foreign to what Ramsey is trying to do in *Religious Language*.

A third thing that may be meant is that religious language is odd in that it is the expression of essentially intractable, a-rational mysteries. It is, in his view, a characteristic of religious commitment that it 'sees in a situation all that the understanding can give us and more'.[21] If this does not mean that the truth-conditions of religious assertions are not exhaustively empirical – the first possibility discussed above – it may mean that religious commitment involves the individual in going beyond any possible sets of truth-conditions, that no possible sets of truth-conditions could entail the 'religious attitude'. A similar view is suggested by further remarks Ramsey makes on the Resurrection, in which it is claimed that despite the fact that it contains empirical con-

[20] Ramsey, op. cit., p. 127.
[21] ibid., p. 17.

ditions that are necessary it cannot be dated, and that to attempt to date the Resurrection is to commit some type or category fallacy. 'We cannot *date* the *Resurrection* : any more than we can walk out with Pythagoras' Theorem or find the square root of love.'[22] Therefore to say 'the third day He rose from the dead' has 'logical impropriety'. It is logically very distinct from a grammatical parallel such as 'The third day he rose again from his bed'.[23] But if an assertion has a set of logically necessary conditions that include events, such as a tomb becoming empty, or, in the case of the Virgin Birth, a conception, it is extremely odd to say that that of which these datable occurrences are the necessary conditions cannot itself be dated. Let it be granted that the biblical language about the Virgin Birth is not exhaustively scientific; it is still partly scientific or empirical in that notions such as 'conceive', a purely physiological notion, are used.

When Ramsey talks of seeing more in a situation than the understanding can give us, if the 'can' here is logical, what this means is that characteristically religious propositions have no conceivable truth-conditions. They are attempts to say the unsayable and so *inevitably* create logical problems. The logical oddity of religious language is then due to the fact that it is an attempt to use language to speak of logical impossibilities, of the inexpressible.

Another phrase Ramsey uses to characterize the distinctiveness of religious language is that the situations that the language refers to are 'perceptual and more' or 'spatio-temporal and more'.[24] Ramsey gives examples, though it is not always clear whether these examples are *cases of* 'perception and more' or just *sufficiently similar to* the only true cases of 'perception and more', namely, religious experiences. One example is of an official and impersonal situation suddenly 'coming alive' when the people involved in it suddenly realize that they know each other.

There is a perfectly familiar sense in which a situation of this kind is 'perceptual and more' in that it involves not only what the people involved in the situation can see and infer from what they see, but also what they believe, i.e. what they 'bring to' the situation in terms of what they believe about themselves, each other, the past, the future and so forth. Similarly when people come to believe in the Resurrection; they may come to believe 'in a flash', but what has happened is that they now believe – for whatever reason, good or bad – that certain propositions are true of the individual denoted by 'Jesus' which previously they believed to be false. But Ramsey may mean that it is perceptual and more in a stronger sense, that it is revealing of some religious truth or insight that can (logically) never properly be articulated.

Part of the difficulty of understanding just what Ramsey means lies in the fact that the word 'disclosure' does double duty. The word is important for him because he believes it to be characteristic of religious experiences that they are disclosures. Sometimes this seems to amount to a claim about the psychology of belief; that while there are many things that we come to believe in bit by bit other things are believed 'in a flash', 'all of a sudden'. The penny drops, the light dawns, and so forth. If this is true, it is a fact about human psychology; it has nothing to do with what makes propositions true, but with how things come to be believed or to be known. On the other hand 'disclosure' seems to refer to an experience of a 'deeper truth' that can only be expressed in or evoked by language that is 'logically odd'.[25]

A fourth thing Ramsey may mean by 'logically odd' is that religious language is like ethical language. This is suggested by the way in which moral judgements figure as examples of logically odd cases throughout the book, and by the stress that is placed upon the fact that, while empirical evidence is relevant to, say, the question whether the Resurrection occurred, no amount of empirical evidence *entails* the occurrence of the Resurrection. (Or is it that no amount of empirical evidence will provide sufficient grounds for someone to come to believe in the Resurrection?) Either way this looks like the often reiterated point about 'is' and 'ought', facts' and 'values'.

'My suggestion is, that "Did the Resurrection occur?", while being no logical kinsman of "Did Queen Anne's death occur?" is logically much more similar to our asking in regard of a certain

---

[25] For a discussion of 'deeper truth' see ibid., pp. 102–3.

situation "Is that a case of duty? Is that a case of genuine personal devotion?" ...

'But in each case the puzzle arises that no amount of "evidence" alone guarantees that in relation to which it is considered, namely, the "Resurrection" on the one hand, or "duty" on the other.

'May not this be because no amount of "evidence" alone can guarantee what exceeds all the evidence taken together: something which is spatio-temporal and more? "Resurrection", like "duty" and "love", all specify occasions – as our examples in Chapter 1 would remind us – for which a whole host of empirical criteria are relevant, but these criteria are organized by, and are never exhaustive evidence for the loyalties they name. None of the criteria in itself guarantees that situation – discernment-response – which exceeds them all.'[26]

The chief difficulty with this interpretation of 'logically odd' is that Ramsey himself seems to reject it in Chapter 2, where he rejects the idea that the Bible records facts which are then interpreted, in favour of the view that the situations to which the Christian appeals are 'ontological peculiars' making distinctive ontological claims.[27]

The purpose of these rather negative remarks on the view that religious language is logically odd is to demonstrate that nothing but confusion can result from treating 'religious language' as one distinctive phenomenon. The unclarity in Ramsey's account is a direct consequence of treating religious language in this *a priori* way, and the several incompatible interpretations that have been offered of his views indicate that, despite the claim that he is giving one consistent view, the phenomena he is dealing with will not allow this. Ramsey may mean that for the religious believer either certain propositions do not have straightforward empirical truth conditions; or that they involve a certain subjective *blik* on the facts; or that they have truth-conditions that it is impossible to conceive; or that they make peculiar moral demands on believers. All these – and perhaps others – are what could be meant by the 'logical oddity' of religious language. But each of these

[26] These passages are taken from ibid., pp. 127–9.
[27] ibid., p. 100.

is a very different thesis. This being so it is surely much more appropriate for a philosopher of religion to defend or attack or examine one or other of these at once, and not to attempt to circumvent these differences by making appeal to 'religious language'.

IV

Another favourite move at present is to say that religious language is typically performative. In an extended treatment of this idea, *Language, Persons and Belief*,[28] Dallas High claims that to say 'I believe' is not to describe but to perform an action, the action, for example, of confessing one's faith. Such a linguistic action is, he claims, 'self-involving'; the performance of the act somehow commits the user to what or who it is that is believed in. Secondly, High makes a sharp distinction between first and third person used of 'believe in'.

'We have seen that to say "I believe in Jones" is to perform an action, i.e. an action of "believing". If someone else says of me "He believes in Jones" something quite different is going on here . . . "He believes . . ." is saying something *about* me and my action. It is a report or assertion about me, what I have done and might well do in the future, viewed as a policy, tendency, or disposition.'[29]

From this point – maintained on doubtful grounds, as will be shown below – High wishes to conclude that because 'I believe' is a claim or a performance, and not a statement, because the man who sincerely says 'I believe that p' does not mistrust his beliefs, to say 'I believe . . .' does make sense and is reasonable. The argument for this conclusion appears to be as follows :

(a) The dichotomies between faith and reason, fact and value, science and religion are wrong.

(b) They are avoidable if attention is paid to the logical peculiarities of the linguistic act of believing.

(c) Belief is indispensable for thinking and talking in general.

[28] New York, 1967.
[29] ibid., p. 158.

'No human intelligence or speech, however original or critical, can function outside the conditions of judgement, personal assent, and the fiduciary modes of human confidence and life. In short, language (and what counts as "knowing") depends upon some sort of "believing", whatsoever form of believing a person or persons (as a culture) may accept.'[30]

(*d*) Hence religious belief, a case of belief, cannot be confined to a conceptually self-contained circle (fideism) but is necessarily linked with reason-giving.

'Saying "I believe" with first-person performative force entails my responsibility and readiness to give reasons for my belief. These reasons are grounds or evidence in support of my belief and may be cited, particularly if I am challenged.'[31]

There are a number of serious confusions in this position, which it is tempting to follow up. However, the remarks that follow are confined to whether what High says contributes at all to understanding religious belief.

Can it be right that to say sincerely 'I believe . . .' is not to state, but to act? Even if it is supposed that asserting is not a linguistic act, which this claim of High's seems to require, and which is dubious, what argument is there to show that when someone sincerely says 'I believe . . .' he is not reporting what he believes? Current unwillingness to say that such an utterance could be a statement is due partly to the desire to say that there is a sharp contrast between reports of states of mind and attitudes, and performatives. No doubt there is. But the contrast is not between performances and states or attitudes but between performatives and statements. Statements do not necessarily report states. It is true that some do : 'Jones has a headache' reports a state of Jones. But 'Jones believes that p' does not describe the goings-on in Jones's head; it does not say whether this belief is a disposition or something that Jones is actively entertaining; whether it is a belief he holds willingly or unwillingly, or whatever.

Likewise when I say 'I believe in Jones' and am thereby stat-

[30] ibid., pp. 140–1.
[31] ibid., p. 209.

ing my belief or attitude I am not reporting my psychological state, but am stating what it is I am believing or believing in.[32] High is right in thinking that when first-person utterances are made they are not necessarily *descriptive* of the person's mental condition, but this does not mean that they are not statements, and are without a truth-value because they are performances or linguistic acts. In places High does acknowledge that the recitations of creeds which he regards as 'linguistic performances of self-involvement'[33] are also concerned with questions of fact and of description.[34] If this is so, it is of the first importance, and while it is fair that a philosopher should neglect one feature of a case to concentrate on others, in this case the fact-stating or putative fact-stating function of religious language cannot be ignored and the 'linguistic acts' be treated as though they do not have truth-values.

To show this, let us grant that the utterances of the creeds are self-involving actions, such as claiming, confessing, expressing loyalty, devotion etc. It is always in order in such cases to ask '*What* is being confessed?' '*To whom* is loyalty being given?' The utterances are not just expressions of loyalty etc. but *propositional* expressions. And if it is in order to ask '*What* is being confessed?', it is also in order to ask '*On what grounds* is it being confessed?' Further, since these questions are askable, are relevant, it is presumably possible to have confessings, expressions of loyalty that conflict with each other or contradict each other. The fact that 'I believe in . . .' is a personal accrediting or a performance, if it is, does not purchase immunity from criticism for it, but is strictly irrelevant to such criticism unless one is going to propose the view that expressions of religious belief are strictly non-propositional in character, and take the consequences philosophically. High allows that 'I believe . . .' is not invulnerable to reason or critical scrutiny. But if it is not invulnerable, what is special about it? High says that my preparedness to say 'I believe' 'means that I do not mistrust . . . my beliefs as connected with the performance of first-person present indicative use'.[35] But what

---

[32] For an excellent discussion of this point in connection with 'knowledge-claims' see Richard Robinson, 'The Concept of Knowledge', *Mind*, (Jan. 1971).

[33] op. cit., p. 175.

[34] op. cit., p. 151.

[35] op. cit., p. 160.

does this show? That to say 'I believe . . .' does make sense and is reasonable, according to High. But what makes a belief reasonable are grounds, reasons, not the fact, if it is a fact, that one cannot mistrust one's own belief. If one is not going to say that religious belief is non-propositional, as High is not, then the point that expressions of religious belief may be a performance of this or that linguistic act is strictly irrelevant to many of the philosophical issues raised by religious beliefs.

In his chapter 'Believing and Giving Reasons' High claims that the distinction between the first- and third-person cases involves a distinction between reasons and causes respectively.

'It is the first-person use of "believe" (e.g. "I believe in Jesus Christ as Lord") that claims company with "reason", "justification", and "responsibility". Construed as a third-person paradigm, we are invited only to see "causes", "explanations", and "dispositions to behaviour" (e.g. "He believes so and so") as answers to questions of "why" one believes.'[36]

We have seen reason enough to doubt this sharp distinction between 'I' and 'he'. But, apart from these reasons, what is there to make us think that there is any philosophically-significant link between 'I believe' and the necessity to give reasons for one's belief and 'He believes' and the necessity to give causes of why he believes? The distinction betwen causal and reason-giving explanations is a familiar one, but it has nothing to do with the person in which claims are made. Of both the first- and third-person cases it can be asked 'Why?' where this question is *either* a request for reasons *or* for causes.

'I believe in Jones.'
'Why?'
'Because he is truthful, trustworthy, loyal etc.' (reasons)
'Because I need to have someone I can trust.' (cause)

'He believes in Jones.'
'Why?'
'Because he is truthful . . .' (reasons)
'Because he needs someone he can lean on.' (cause)

[36] op. cit., p. 203.

The symmetry between these cases is obvious. Nor is there any conceptual link between avowing a belief and being prepared to support it with reasons. Preparedness to do this depends on what sort of belief is being avowed.

The philosophical moral to be drawn from this tangle of confusions is that it is disastrous to try to cut through a series of separate issues by an appeal to a supposed distinctive feature of religious language. Some of the separate issues are : Is religious language used to do characteristic things? What, if religious language is used to do characteristic things, is the relation between this fact and the meaning, in the sense of sense and reference, of the expression so used? What reasons are/can be given to justify religious beliefs? Even supposing that religious language is used characteristically to do certain things, it does not follow that it is never used to do other things. Nor does it follow that what it is used to do can be considered independently of the propositions involved. Nor does it follow that to indicate its characteristic uses is to provide grounds for the reasonableness of the belief.

v

The purpose of discussing these examples of popular moves in the philosophy of religion is not to argue that they are all misconceived, nor to dispute the claim that there is something distinctive about religion marking it off from, say, science or politics, nor that such a view of religion as Phillips's is not a *possible* one. The discussion has been with the purpose of making an essentially simple methodological point : that to appeal to what the believer says cannot provide indisputable premises for arguments in the philosophy of religion, and that attempts to display the supposedly distinctive 'logic' of religious language do not succeed. Both programmes founder for the same basic reason : the idea that there is some necessary, unique uniformity in religious belief and religious talk.

The next chapters will demonstrate that no such uniformity exists, by looking at certain distinct accounts of religious belief.

4

BELIEF AND KNOWLEDGE

Words such as 'belief', 'know' and 'knowledge' are not used univocally in English. They have different meanings which sometimes are, sometimes are not, accurately reflected in ordinary usage. There are also pairs of contrasts such as 'knowledge by acquaintance' and 'knowledge by description', and 'belief in' and 'belief that' that figure in a key way in some accounts of religious epistemology. It is the purpose of this chapter to sketch some of the conceptual differences between the notions mentioned. This exercise is necessary before different models of belief can be considered, for in most of these, though not all, the conceptual differences to be discussed here are reflected. It would appear that philosophical and theological discussion of religious belief has in some cases been consciously modelled on some general concept of belief; religious belief has been taken to be a species of some genus.

I

To begin, three different senses of belief or knowledge will be distinguished. The locution 'belief or knowledge' is used deliberately to avoid any appeal to usage in distinguishing these cases, and in two of the three it is quite possible for someone, on the grounds of usage, to say that they are cases of belief, others that they are cases of knowledge. Further, the alternative ways of characterizing these uses help as a reminder that it is not necessary to say that any one of them is superior to any of the others. What matters is that these three senses are distinguishable, and that they are all plausible cases of knowledge or belief.

(*a*) There is a sense of 'know' which in ordinary use is not contrasted with 'believe' : what H. H. Price has called the 'wider sense'.[1] Price appears to mean that 'know' in this sense implies

[1] 'Some Considerations about Belief', *P.A.S.*, 1934–5. Reprinted in A. P. Griffiths ed. *Knowledge and Belief* (1967), p. 41ff.

subjective certainty that p, but that it does not entail the truth of p. That is, in this wide sense 'Jones knows that p' implies that Jones is more convinced of the truth of p than he would be if he were to say 'I believe that p'. Because 'know' in this sense does not entail the truth of what is known, it is more likely that its use will be in the first person. It is in this sense of 'know' that most unreflective, everyday claims to knowledge are made, such as 'I know that my wife is in the kitchen', 'I know that there are hydrangeas in the garden', and so forth.

(b) At the other end of the scale is the sense of 'know' in which nothing could count against the claim that one knows p, and it is in this sense of the three discussed here that 'belief' would not be an appropriate alternative verb, because of the possibilities of correction that are implied by its use. The point about this case is not that as a matter of fact there is no evidence against p, but, as Norman Malcolm points out, when someone claims that he knows p in this sense he refuses to admit that the proposition p could turn out to be false. Investigation into the 'evidence' for the truth or falsity of p is not in place because, at least in the case of analytic propositions, what is known is that some proposition is true in virtue of its meaning, and not in virtue of the way the world is.

Other philosophers have claimed to know sense-data, in this strong sense, and logically to construct, or reconstruct the external world out of them. Malcolm[2] extends this strong sense of 'know' to certain propositions about the external world, those that the knower does not require further evidence to establish the truth of other than what he directly perceives. That is, according to Malcolm, there is a class of propositions which no further evidence could show that one was mistaken about the truth of. Though this is not the place to contest Malcolm's claim, one or two comments call for clarification.

The example of such a proposition as Malcolm gives is a puzzling one. He says that he knows (in the strong sense being discussed) that there is an ink-bottle in front of him now. He admits that the ink-bottle could disappear in the next moment, or

---

[2] 'Knowledge and Belief' in Griffiths, op. cit., p. 69. This is a revised version of the paper that originally appear in *Mind* (1952).

that when he reaches for it his hand should seem to pass through it. Yet because he *knows now* that the bottle is there he is prepared to invite someone in the next room to come and get it. It might be thought that what Malcolm should say is that he *knows* that the bottle is there now, but cannot vouch for what will happen to it in the next minute. All that he seems to be doing is adopting the convention of referring to the existence of material objects where phenomenalists have referred to sense data.

But this would be a mistaken view of what Malcolm is saying. The change is not concerned simply with the conventions of speaking, for Malcolm wants to claim that the bottle *exists* now, no matter what may happen to it or to him in the next few seconds.[3] That is, he appeals to the principle that 'For it to be possible that any statements about physical things should *turn out to be false* it is necessary that some statements about physical things *cannot* turn out to be false'.[4]

This idea of Malcolm's is obviously similar to the position taken by G. E. Moore in his 'Proof of an External World', and it may seem to be similar to Wittgenstein's position on scepticism. This is not so, however, and the difference between Moore and Malcolm on the one hand, and Wittgenstein on the other, can be brought out in the following way. Malcolm and Moore treat certain propositions as obviously true, self-evidently so. But Wittgenstein claims that in the case of certain propositions the idea of evidence, even self-evidence, is not relevant or appropriate. Such propositions are *groundless*, not in the sense of being arbitrary or whimsical, but as themselves providing the grounds or standards for what is to count as knowledge. They are not therefore true in any sense in which evidence is appropriate, but the acceptance of some such propositions provides the basis of judging, assessing and so forth.[5]

[3] op. cit., pp. 76–7.

[4] ibid., p. 78. Compare G. E. Moore 'If those propositions were not certain, then nothing of the kind is ever certain : if *they* were not certain, then no proposition which implies the existence of anything external to the mind of the person who makes it is ever certain.' 'Certainty' in *Philosophical Papers* (Collier Books), p. 239.

[5] Cf. The review of *On Certainty* by Ilham Dilman in *Philosophy* (April 1971).

'To say of a man, in Moore's sense, that he *knows* something; that what he says is therefore unconditionally the truth, seems wrong to me. – It is the truth only inasmuch as it is an unmoving foundation of his language-games.'

'That is to say, the *questions* that we raise and our *doubts* depend on the fact that some propositions are exempt from doubt, are as it were like hinges on which those turn.'

'If I ask someone "what colour do you see at the moment?", in order, that is, to learn what colour is there at the moment, I cannot at the same time question whether the person I ask understands English, whether he wants to take me in, whether my own memory is not leaving me in the lurch as to the names of colours, and so on.'[6]

What is being said here is that within a given, working language-game grammatical questions about that language-game cannot be raised. The sense in which, in a given language-game, certain propositions must be certain and must be known throws light on the sense in which those who take a 'strict autonomist' view of religious belief think of the existence of God as being certain and known for the participant, i.e. the religious believer.

A second puzzle with Malcolm's account concerns his claim that 'If I make an assertion of the form "I know that p" it does not follow that p, whether or not I am using "know" in the strong sense'. This seems to go against the drift of Malcolm's earlier discussion which appeared to say that a person would not utter 'I know that p' (in the strong sense) unless p were true. The example he gives is puzzling. 'If I have said to someone outside my room "Of course, I know that Freddie is in here", and I am speaking in the strong sense, it does not *follow* that Freddie is where I claim he is.'[7] But this is just the sort of case in which I could not be using 'know' in the strong sense, a case in which I think that there is someone in another room. Or is using 'know' in the strong sense simply a matter of *thinking* that p, the object of (strong) knowledge could not turn out to be false?[8]

The exact relation between Malcolm, Moore and Wittgen-

---

[6] *On Certainty* (1969) paras. 403, 341, 345.
[7] Malcolm in Griffiths ed., op. cit., p. 81.
[8] Wittgenstein says similar things in *On Certainty*, e.g. para. 137.

stein on these questions is a complex and controversial one. Fortunately, it need not detain us here. It is necessary only to make the point that it is at least plausible that some of these philosophers claim that the strong sense of know/believe is not confined to analytic propositions or propositions about sense-data, but that some at least of the propositions about the external world are known in the strong sense.

(c) A third sense of know/believe is that ordinarily analysed as justified, true belief. As A. J. Ayer puts it, 'the necessary and sufficient conditions for knowing that something is the case are first that what one is said to know be true, secondly that one be sure of it, and thirdly that one should have the right to be sure'.[9] This right might be based on the evidence of one's own senses, or on testimony, and the right is a right to ignore further evidence on the grounds that it would be unreasonable to entertain the supposition that the proposition believed could be false. A person could be said to know in this sense when, although the proposition could have been other than it is, he has it on good authority that the proposition is true. Despite the analysis of know/believe in this sense in terms of belief, truth and justification 'A knows/believes that p' does not entail p, for it is logically possible that not-p. What is entailed is a knowledge *claim*, or action as if it were logically impossible that not-p. It might seem odd that this sense of know is also called belief, but many philosophers have wanted to deny that a corrigible proposition could be known with certainty. Locke took this position and regarded religious beliefs as a species of belief in this sense.[10]

[9] *The Problem of Knowledge* (1956), p. 35.

[10] Though Locke does speak of 'degrees' of knowledge. On this see J. Yolton, *Locke and the Compass of Human Understanding* (1970), ch. 3. There are difficulties with the analysis of knowledge as justified, true, belief. The main one is that, since it is possible to have identical beliefs and justifications for contradictory propositions, no one is ever in a position, on this analysis of knowledge, to know that he knows. Edmund L. Gettier's well-known objection to this analysis arises partly from this feature. For someone who wishes to maintain this analysis, or something like it, the Gettier paradox will have to be surmounted by building in other conditions, such as those suggested by Roderick Chisholm. Of course the Gettier objection does not stand if knowledge is analysed differently. It does not stand, for example, in the Malcolm case just discussed, or in the model of religious belief to be examined in chapter 5. (See Edmund L. Gettier 'Is justified true belief knowledge?', *Analysis*, 1963 and Roderick M. Chisholm, *Theory of Knowledge* (1966), p.23n.)

II

As we saw in the last case, it has been customary to analyse knowledge as a complex of three necessary and jointly sufficient conditions – belief, truth, and evidence or grounds, conveying the 'right to be sure'. Some uses of 'know' pick up two of the three conditions, other uses another two. A person may say that he knows p where he believes p and has grounds for his belief; for example, the claim that the sun will rise tomorrow, or claims to know any future contingent proposition, are in this category. Further, a person may be said to know when he believes p and p is true but where the grounds for p, though generally accessible, are not accessible to him, or where he is not in a position, though he knows the grounds, to evaluate them. An example would be knowing that p on the view of experts, or a child's knowledge of a proposition.

Let us give the name 'ideological knowledge' to the case where p is believed/known, where the believer has grounds for his belief, i.e. it is not merely a guess or a hunch, but where the grounds are of such a character that they are not universally acceptable, though they are acceptable to the believer's co-ideologists, and are of such a form that someone who is not of this ideological persuasion could say 'If I were of your persuasion, x, y and z would be good grounds for p'.

There are a number of reasons why knowledge claims are not generally accepted, apart from the central one that they do not have sufficient evidence to support them. Some of these are:

(a) Where what is believed is a contingent proposition about the world, it may be disputed on the grounds that it has been misunderstood or misinterpreted. That is, a distinction is made between *fact* and *interpretation*. People may be said to differ in their ideological claims when they agree on some of the facts in a particular case, but differ in their interpretations. That is, they have certain descriptions in common, but disagree on other descriptions, and/or on the significance to be attached to them. The impression is often given that such differences, sometimes called differences in 'evaluation', necessarily involve some inner sense, or feelings, or that they have to do with 'values', not 'facts'.

But such a view is not implied here : it is sufficient for differences in ideological knowledge-claims that there are differences in beliefs between the individuals making them. They differ in the *grounds* they offer in support of the knowledge-claims they make. To interpret 'the facts' differently is to fit knowledge, or beliefs held in common, into different and incompatible patterns of belief.

(*b*) Where what is believed is not fully understood. The objection here will be about the meaning of the proposition. For instance, if Smith claims to know a proposition of the form 'God is . . .' then Jones might object on the grounds that 'God' denotes an individual that is, at best, not fully comprehensible. Disputes of this kind have bred familiar arguments about theological predication, and have led to the claim that through a proposition of the form 'God is . . .' cannot be known, because it cannot fully be comprehended, yet it is certain (where 'certain' is defined epistemically). Claims of this sort will be examined in Chapter 6.

(*c*) Where what is believed is based on some private experience or experiences, and so is not teachable. 'Private' here does not mean 'logically private' but 'individual'. If a person or group of people claim to have experienced God (in some way) then the most they can hope to do is to provide directions and training to enable others to experience him, as with anything fairly recondite. 'Unteachability' here refers to contingent barriers in the way of verifying experiences or putative experiences. More generally relevant to teachability in this sense is whether having a reason for a belief entails being able to give it. For being able to give a reason is a necessary condition for teaching certain propositions. If having a reason for a belief does not entail being able to give a reason, then propositions whose truth cannot be taught in this way are not *ipso facto* irrational.[11]

III

The fact that there are such different cases of 'know' is the reason for the sometimes confusing semantics of epistemology, including (and especially perhaps) religious epistemology. Because 'know'

[11] On the verification of religious experience, and the connection between having and giving reasons see George I. Mavrodes, *Belief in God* (1970), p. 11ff, p. 73ff.

in the strict sense carries with it the entailment that what is known is true, the word comes to be used in much less strict circumstances. As J. L. Austin and others have pointed out, 'know' has this 'honorific' connotation that carries with it the idea of a personal guarantee.

On the other hand the reason why 'believe' is more apt in certain circumstances is that one cannot, for instance, speak of strengths of knowledge, but only of strengths of belief, or of strengths in the cogency of the *grounds* for knowledge. So that where a person is unsure either of the grounds or of the truth of his belief he may say that he believes p, whereas in fact he may know p in the sense that p may be true, and his belief that p may be justified. Another reason for using 'belief' instead of 'knowledge' might be political. Given a state where (i) there is a plurality of religions and (ii) the state is neutral with respect to all of them, such religions will be referred to in the constitution as embodying 'beliefs' or 'opinions'. But this political fact does not have any philosophical consequences for religion or theology. So there may be good psychological and political reasons for using 'belief' in preference to 'knowledge' in a variety of circumstances.

Again, a person may use 'believe' not when he is not absolutely sure but when he is sure, yet cannot show conclusively that he has the right to be sure. Price says that belief and knowledge are contrasted when 'know' is used in the sense of absolutely certain. But this does not seem necessarily to be the case, for a person can believe with absolute certainty that p even though he cannot give the grounds for p. 'Belief' is not always used in a concessive sense implying a lack of certainty. It may be, but its use may be due to the fact that what is lacking is not certainty but proof. No doubt 'believe' is often used in opposition to 'know', as a guarded, concessive way of speaking : guarded, because 'believe' does not entail the truth of what is believed. Yet this is not a necessary feature of religious belief, for a case will be discussed in Chapter 6 in which, though belief is contrasted with knowledge, this is not because belief does not entail truth but rather that the type and availability of grounds for belief are not such as to warrant the claim to know. Though belief is contrasted with knowledge, on this view religious belief is a case of true belief :

'A religiously believes p' entails 'A truly believes p', whereas on the Locke-Butler view (to be discussed in Chapter 5) 'A religiously believes p' entails only 'A believes p justifiably'.

Another way of putting the point about ideological knowledge would be to say that A ideologically knew p where A was (subjectively) certain as to p and where he gave reasons for p, but where the reasons for p were using premisses not generally acceptable. This is to be distinguished from sheer irrationality, where *no* grounds are offered for p, and from the case where generally acceptable, but weak, grounds are given – i.e. where the grounds are strong enough to warrant belief that p, but not strong enough to warrant the claim to know that p, in a non-ideological sense of 'know'.

As with knowledge and belief, ambiguity infects 'certain'. Briefly, four cases can be discussed.

(*a*) 'Certain' can refer to a feeling. Smith's feeling of certainty does not entail the truth of what he feels certain about. This use can be discarded as of no epistemological interest. Likewise with avowals. From 'I am certain that p' it does not follow that p is certain.

(*b*) A second case is where 'p is certain' entails 'p is true' but not 'p is known'.

(*c*) 'Certain' can be used as an epistemic term. Whether or not Moore is right in saying 'a thing that nobody knows may quite well be true, but cannot possibly be certain' is disputable. It might be claimed, as above, that if p is true then it follows that it is certain. But no matter. We can *make* 'certain' an epistemic term. If we do, then 'p is certain' entails 'p is known' which in turn entails 'p is true'.

It is true that a necessary condition of someone truly *asserting* 'It is certain that p' is that p is known by the asserter, but not that for the *proposition* 'It is certain that p' to be true it must be known.

(*d*) A fourth case is where the *assertion* 'p is certain' entails 'p is true' but not 'p is known'. Where, that is, '–(–p epistemologically impossible)' can be truly asserted, and where the grounds for this are stronger than probabilifying grounds, but less strong than the grounds that give knowledge, if a necessary condition for knowledge is the ability to demonstrate the truth of what is known.

The fact that 'A is certain that p' entails p rules out this sense of certainty being synonymous with belief in any sense of 'belief' that does not entail the truth of what is believed. And the fact that grounds, though not demonstrable grounds, can be given for it means that it is not simply a case of guesswork. Because of the necessary dependence of this sense of 'certain' on some authority whose word can be taken for things, the locution 'It is certain that p' will only be used by those accepting the authority, and hence the truth of p. Those not accepting the authority, and hence not accepting the entailment of p by 'It is certain that p', will not describe the case in these terms at all.

The setting out of these different notions of belief, knowledge and certainty does not imply that whichever is accepted is a matter of sheer indifference. No doubt it is widely denied that what we have called 'ideological knowledge' is a case of knowledge; and many claim that, properly speaking, the knowledge-claims we make are only refutable conjectures. Some will deny that there are cases of epistemic certainty that are not cases of knowledge.

'If someone cannot give the grounds for his claim to be sure of p then we had better withdraw it.' But this is not the place to develop and discuss such criticisms. What is of interest here is the fact that there are such concepts and that ordinary usage of verbs such as 'know' and 'believe' reflects these. 'So much the worse for ordinary language' is a fair retort but the argument justifying such different concepts is not based on an ordinary language 'appeal' but on the adequacy or otherwise of the characterizations of these notions that has been offered. What is of importance for this study is that people use 'know' and 'believe' in these ways and that such usage is not obviously incoherent.

IV

When is believing a proposition also a case of believing a person? To many writers on religion at present this will seem an odd question, because it has been customary to make a sharp distinction between 'person' and 'propositional' knowledge. It is alleged that 'personal' knowledge involves 'commitment' and consists in an 'I – thou' relation, while propositional knowledge is 'objective', 'theoretical', 'detached' and so forth. There are a number of different strands to this sort of claim, only some of which will be examined now.[12] *A priori* at least there seems to be little reason for such a sharp disjunction.

There is no antithesis between believing a proposition and believing a person, if the proposition concerned is understood to be the assertion of some person. For A to believe B, B must assert p and A must believe p. The locution 'Jones believes Smith' is often just an abbreviation for 'Jones believes what Smith asserts'.

In the case of 'know' matters are different. While it makes sense to ask what the conditions are for believing p to be believing Smith, the question 'Under what conditions is knowing that p a case of knowing Smith?' has no clear sense. Under no conditions is knowing p a case of knowing a person, though to know a person it seems necessary to be able to say something about the person, to formulate part of one's knowledge in propositions, though in fact this ability may never be exercised. No amount of knowings-that-p will add up to knowing a person, because knowing a person is a state that is untransferrable and (with certain marginal exceptions) immediate. To know Smith, Jones must know Smith for himself. Smith cannot be known for Jones by Robinson.

For someone whose sole means of knowledge on a subject was the testimony of others, every case of believing a proposition on that subject (apart from inferences made from propositions known) would also be a case of believing the one who asserted that p. This is another reason by propositions that come to be known exclusively through testimony are appropriately called 'beliefs', because they involve believing another person. This is not to say that the logical features of such beliefs are identical with beliefs in the sense of hypotheses. A major purpose of later chapters is to bring out these different logical features in the case of different models of religious belief.

What is the difference between believing in (in the sense of

---

[12] Other strands are discussed in the present writer's 'Revealed Propositions and Timeless Truths' *Religious Studies* (June 1972).

trusting) Jones and believing Jones? There is a logical distinction in that it is possible to believe Jones without regarding him as generally trustworthy. The question 'Do you believe in Jones?', as a question about the existence of Jones, cannot presuppose the existence of Jones. But it does as a question about trusting Jones.

Believing can be restricted to an isolated proposition, believing that today is Tuesday, for example. To say this is isolated is not to say that it does not have many implications. But believing in, in the sense of trusting (and not in the sense of believing in the existence of), must refer to a range of acts or dispositions, unless the verb is qualified, as 'I believe in him when I can see him'. Believing, insofar as it concerns another person, refers to what he says, while believing-in covers both his words and deeds, and the 'roles' that he plays or is capable of playing. And believing covers past or present assertions only, while belief-in covers past and future, though the grounds of such trust can only be past. Thus it is odd to say 'I believe whatever he is about to say' (unless I know what he is about to say because he has told me) unless it is the case that I believe in him. It follows from this that A can be believed in if – and only if – A has a character, and does not represent a random series.

Earlier a distinction was made between belief in the existence of, and belief in the reliability of, a person. Believing in Jones's reliability obviously implies belief in the existence of Jones. But belief-in does not carry existential import in all cases. When what is believed in is regarded as a non-existent but possible and desirable state of affairs, believing in that state of affairs is compatible with its non-existence. To believe in God is different from believing in votes for women. To believe in God is not to believe that God would be a good thing, whereas to believe in votes for women is to believe that votes for women would be a good thing. To believe in God is (at least) to believe in the existence of God. Where the existence of God is taken for granted, to say that one believes in God is tantamount to saying that one has a certain affective attitude towards God, though some – e.g. Norman Malcolm – argue that to believe in God is both to believe that God exists and to have a certain affective attitude to God, such as love or fear, and that this is one crucial respect in which belief in God differs from belief in material objects.[13] The parallel between believing in God and believing in ideals holds just here, in that whether belief-in is used in contexts that carry existential import or not, it involves the having of certain dispositions, usually favourable ones, to what is believed in.[14]

Let us turn to consider the difference between 'belief-in' and trust. 'Jones believes in God' entails that 'Jones believes that God exists', but it certainly does not entail that God exists. What of 'trust'? Does 'Jones trusts A' entail the existence of A? The answer to this is that it depends in what respect Jones trusts A. If he trusts a plank across a stream then the object of the verb is non-intensional in character. To trust the plank is not primarily to have certain beliefs about the characteristics of the plank, but to act with respect to the plank in certain ways, believing or hoping that the plank will be safe. The existential import of 'trust' often depends on whether what follows the verb is or is not a referring expression. The 'trust' in 'He trusts in a plank' often does not carry existential import because 'plank' does not necessarily refer to a particular plank. For a similar reason the agnostic prefers to talk of other people's belief in *a* God rather than belief in God.

Trust requires beliefs, though it is not necessarily a form of belief, but a disposition to act in certain ways. (This applies to 'trust in' and not 'trust that'. 'Trust that' seems to be a non-strict use of 'trust'.) So to trust in the plank is to act in certain ways with respect to the plank, believing that such and such. To trust in God is to act with respect to God in certain ways believing that such and such. But to trust in God does not entail that God exists, for it is possible to trust in God under the mistaken impression that he exists, just as one can trust in the government under the mistaken impression that it exists, the Prime Minister having just handed in his resignation.

In the paper referred to earlier, Malcolm makes the point that for the believer in God the question of the existence of God is not something that can be considered independently of his belief. This seems to be truer of 'trust in' than 'believe in'. For, as has

[13] 'Is it a Religious Belief that "God exists"?' in John Hick ed., *Faith and the Philosophers* (1964).

[14] Cf. J. J. Macintosh, 'Belief-in', *Mind* (July 1970).

been shown, 'belief in' is ambiguous between 'believe in the existence of' and 'trust', so that it is possible to raise the question of
whether someone believes in the existence of God, independently
of raising the question of whether he trusts God. But 'trusts in' is
not ambiguous in a parallel way, and the question of whether
someone trusts in God cannot be raised independently of the
question of whether he believes in God. It may be that the *belief that God exists*, as against the *belief in God* is, as Malcolm
says, a 'problematic concept', and that this is due historically to
thinking of the existence of God as something that has *grounds*,
which, together with the idea of the existence of God, could be
accepted independently of affective states or attitudes. It may
be that in the case of a Jewish or Christian conception of God
one could not believe that he exists and 'not be touched at all
by awe or dismay or fear'.[15] But it is still the case that there are
forms of belief in God in which it makes sense to make the separation. Certain forms of deism would be an example, in which
God is conceived of as the source of all that is, and the upholder
of all that is, but not as a redeemer or judge.

A final remark on this. The thesis that one cannot *believe* in
the existence of God independently of having certain affective
states towards God is inclined to become the thesis that the
existence of such a God cannot be discussed. But the question,
Does the God whom to believe in is to love/fear/be in dread of
etc. exist? seems to be perfectly meaningful. If meaningful, it
is logically possible to answer it by giving *grounds*. As a matter
of fact, there may be no such grounds, because, as Malcolm suggests, there may be no agreed-on good or bad reasons for believing in the God whom to believe in is to fear. This means that any
discussion of the grounds will fall flat. But it does not mean that
some people will agree together that x, y and z are good grounds,
and that others agree that a, b and c are good grounds. Nor,
further, that because the second group does not find the grounds
satisfied, it does not believe, while the first group finds them
satisfied, and does believe. (This is the sort of situation envisaged
earlier when certain claims to know were referred to as 'ideological'; they have grounds, but not generally-agreed-on grounds.)

[15] Malcolm, op. cit., p. 107.

V

All the cases of knowledge so far discussed have been cases of knowledge by description, except perhaps the Malcolm case, where one of the conditions of knowledge was that the knower had to be in the presence of what was known. Yet even this condition was not a universal requirement of Malcolm's examples. In this section the distinction betwen knowledge by acquaintance and knowledge by description will be examined, particularly because of the fact that a recent attempt to analyse religious belief makes use of the notion of knowledge by acquaintance. This attempt by John Hick will be examined below, in Chapter 8.

The basic distinction is made by Russell in *The Problems of Philosophy*, and in his paper 'Knowledge by Acquaintance and Knowledge by Description' published in 1910.[16] He used the distinction for the purposes of maintaining the possibility of the intuition of sensations, knowledge of universals, and logical truths. Whatever may be the plausibility or otherwise of this view it corresponds to a loose but widely-held distinction about knowledge in general. Bernard Mayo in *The Logic of Personality*[17] has disputed whether acquaintance is what Russell means here, and whether he would not have been more correct to have given a different label to the distinction, and also whether the inappropriateness of 'knowledge by acquaintance' does not indicate wider epistemological difficulties in Russell's work. This may be so. Whether it is or not, the distinction itself has been given wider applications.

Suppose Jones says to a friend 'The Smiths have got a cook you'll be glad to know'.[18] He could mean 'You'll be glad to know that the Smiths have got a cook' or 'You'll be glad to know the cook that the Smiths have got'. In the case of the first gloss, what Jones's friend will be glad to know is a *truth*, that the proposition 'The Smiths have a cook' is true. In the second, what it is that Jones's friend will be glad to know is a *person*, the cook

---

[16] *P.A.S.* (1910–11). Reprinted in *Mysticism and Logic* (1917).
[17] 1952, ch. 2.
[18] I owe this example to Edna Johnson.

recently acquired by the Smiths. His knowing the truth that the Smiths have a new cook is due to being told on good authority. But he does not know the new cook as a result of being told that the Smiths have a new cook. (Compare also the ambiguity of 'knowing who' and 'knowing what'.)

'Know' as used in 'knowledge by acquaintance' is a relational expression. Smith knows Jones may be presented as SkJ. What or whom Smith knows is representable by a name, 'Jones'. But such a representation is impossible in the case of knowledge by description. What Smith knows when he knows that Jones is a rascal is not representable by a name but by a proposition. And in knowing that Jones is a rascal Smith does not know by acquaintance the proposition 'Jones is a rascal'.

It may seem obvious that what is known by acquaintance is something non-propositional, a nameable individual. When Jones knows Smith he knows the individual Smith, not a set or propositions. But Hintikka has argued that knowledge by acquaintance is a propositional attitude differing from belief, say, only in that what is known by acquaintance is known directly.[19]

If Jones knows Smith and Smith is the President of the Chamber of Commerce then it follows that Jones knows the President of the Chamber of Commerce. But it does not follow that because he knows the President of the Chamber of Commerce he knows that Smith is the President of the Chamber of Commerce, or that he knows him *as* the President of the Chamber of Commerce. This would only follow when 'Smith' and 'the President of the Chamber of Commerce' refers to the same individual not simply in fact but in all those possible worlds that are compatible with what and who Jones knows.

The distinction between knowledge by description and knowledge by acquaintance is not clearly reflected in the idiomatic contrast between knowledge *of* and knowledge *about*, for there are cases of knowing-of that are cases of knowing about. 'I know of a man who will cut your hair for ten pence' does not reveal of itself whether the man who will cut hair for ten pence is someone whom the speaker is acquainted with, or simply that this is a useful piece of information that someone has passed on to him.

[19] Jaakko Hintikka 'Knowledge by Acquaintance – Individuation by Acquaintance', in *Bertrand Russell*, ed. D. F. Pears (1972).

The remark was made earlier that there does not seem to be any basis for the distinction betwen propositional and personal knowledge that is sometimes met with in religious writings. We can see also that there is no basis for calling knowledge by acquaintance personal *and not* propositional knowledge. Rather, the contrast is between direct and indirect knowledge. Being acquainted with an individual entails knowing *some* truths about that individual, but to be acquainted with an individual is not the same thing as knowing certain truths about him. Further, the truths that are entailed by knowing an individual need not be any particular set of truths, and certainly not all truths. The problems here are analogous to those involving the giving of individuating descriptions; different sets of descriptions may enable the same individual to be picked out from his fellows, just as acquaintance with an individual can give rise to two entirely different sets of descriptions in answer to the question, asked of two different people, 'What can you tell me about your acquaintance Jones?'.

How is an expression such as 'I know Jones' to be understood? If I know Jones I know something about Jones; knowledge by acquaintance involves knowledge by description, but not *vice versa*. What more to knowledge by acquaintance is there than this? Whatever more there is can be nothing peculiar to people, because inanimate things can be known, and non-human animals; things with a few features, like a tie-pin, and with many features, like an old country house. In fact anything that can form part of a person's immediate environment can be known by acquaintance. Just where one's environment ends is problematical, no doubt (if I have only ever talked to a person on the telephone, am I acquainted with him, or not?) but not in any way that affects this present account.

Is immediateness a necessary feature of acquaintance? If by acquaintance is meant some social relationship, then it is difficult to say what the relation between acquaintance and immediateness is. 'I am immediately aware of A but I am not acquainted with A' is not a self-contradiction, nor is 'I am not immediately aware of A but I am acquainted with him'. I may see a man on his way to work each day for ten years, and not be able to list him among my acquaintances. And I may be acquainted with

Peter of whom it is impossible for me to be immediately aware because he is in Australia.

But if by 'acquaintance' is meant something more strictly epistemological, then the point about knowledge by acquaintance is that it is not exhausted by a knowledge of certain *de facto* identities. To say that A is acquainted with B is to say that A is able to pick B out, as a unique individual, placeable by A in a framework of direct knowledge. To know B by acquaintance is to be familiar with B.[20] Becoming acquainted (in the 'social' sense) with B may be a process that is uninterrupted until the time that the knower avows that he knows B, or the process of becoming acquainted with B may cease before the avowal. But if the avowal is true, then it is necessarily the case that at some time there has been a process of getting acquainted with B. Just as getting to know someone can be a process, so knowing someone by acquaintance is a matter of degree, for one can know someone better or poorly, whereas knowing that such and such is true is not a process, though getting to know that it is true may be. Knowing by acquaintance is a matter of degree but it has a clear necessary condition, becoming familiar with by being in the presence of and talking to and being addressed by the one concerned. The reason why knowledge by acquaintance is nontransferable is not because all cases of knowing by acquaintance are immediate but because of the familiarity condition. If Jones was acquainted with Smith and could tell Robinson all that he knew about Smith, it would not follow that Robinson was acquainted with Smith, simply because he has never been familiar with him.

VI

It was stated rather summarily at the beginning of this chapter that belief is a propositional attitude. What this means depends on what 'proposition' is taken to mean. The purpose of this note is to draw atttention to two of the things it could mean that are relevant to the discussion of religious belief.

(*a*) It could mean simply that what is believed are statements or assertions. That is, to believe p is simply to take p for true.

[20] Hintikka, op. cit.

F

Geach has pointed out the ambiguity between statement as a word that refers to what a truth-value can be assigned to, and as the speech-act of stating.[21] In this sense of propositional belief, then, what are believed are what are asserted as being true.

(*b*) It could mean that what is believed are propositional functions, forms of words in which things are propounded for consideration. This is how Geach explains what he means by 'proposition', but it is not very perspicuous, because 'propounded for consideration' could itself be a speech-act, and Geach wants sharply to distinguish this sense of proposition from linguistic acts of any sort. But his point can be put differently; while 'proposition' in his sense has a truth-value the fact that it has a truth-value does not entail that it is being asserted, or propounded as true. It may be, for example, a component part of a disjunction, or a question, or a command, and these are not assertions. 'Believe' is not a very good word to characterize a general attitude to propositions in this second sense, because to believe is to take for true, and commands, questions etc. are not what are taken for true. It makes no sense to talk of believing commands or questions. A word like 'assent' which covers not only beliefs but also a range of 'propositional attitudes' would be better, but even this would not cover questions, for example.

It is not necessary to do more than point out this ambiguity here. Some further features of the problem are discussed in the chapter on belief as assent.

²¹ 'Assertion', *Philosophical Review* (October 1965).

PART II

5

PROBABILITY

The fourth sense of know/believe outlined in Chapter 4 is the view that a contingent proposition is believed when there are grounds which justify it. These grounds, though not demonstrably conclusive, are nevertheless generally accessible, in a way in which the grounds for 'ideological' knowledge claims are not. To some philosophers such propositions, if the grounds for them give 'the right to be sure', are instances of knowledge, and not merely of belief. A. J. Ayer in *The Problem of Knowledge* is a case of someone who takes this view. This present chapter will be devoted to developing a model of religious belief as a species of belief/knowledge in this sense. On this view 'belief' in 'religious belief' is an epistemic word, and religious belief is a case of what Locke called 'assured' belief – belief that *operationally* cannot be distinguished from those basic intuitions and deductive certainties which were for him the only cases of true knowledge. The model will be developed using Locke, Butler and F. R. Tennant as examples.

Because in this case it is possible for someone to be justified in believing what is in fact false, the Gettier counter-examples to knowledge (analysed as justified, true belief) briefly alluded to in Chapter 4, are counter-examples to this view. Their existence would not, however, worry Locke or Butler, for, as will appear, for them religious belief is essentially practical. That there are theoretical objections to this account of belief, such as Gettier's, or the sceptic's, is irrelevant to its religious value and function.

I

In Chapter 10 of Book IV of the *Essay* Locke claims that the existence of God is demonstrable by inference from the knowledge a man has of himself.

From the consideration of ourselves and what we infallibly find
in our own constitutions, our reason leads us to the knowledge of
this certain and evident truth : that *there is an eternal, most
powerful, and most knowing being*, which whether anyone will
please to call *God*, it matters not.[1]

That is, Locke claims that we know that God exists (in the strong
sense of know) as surely as we know that we exist. 'We have a
more certain knowledge of the existence of a God than of anything our senses have not immediately discovered to us.'

For Locke, as for Descartes, God's existence is a matter of
knowledge, not of belief. But there are many other religious propositions that can only be believed, and it is on these that this
chapter concentrates. What distinguishes a religious belief from
any other sort of belief is that it has a religious meaning. Such
beliefs are not, for Locke, confined to the propositions of natural
theology, but include revealed propositions, though revealed in
a pretty attenuated sense, as we shall see.

Locke's epistemology is characterized throughout by a sharp
contrast between knowledge and belief. Contingent truths can
only be believed; because they could be false, they cannot
be known (with absolute certainty) to be true. Historical propositions, for example, are only probably true, and so it is possible
only to have beliefs about the past, not knowledge. Insofar as
propositions with a religious meaning have a corrigible component they can only at best be probably true, and can only
be believed, not known.

In fact there is no entailment here. That is to say :

(*a*) Some religious propositions are about the past.

(*b*) Propositions about the past are only probably true.

do not entail

(*c*) No religious propositions about the past can be known
to be certainly true.

There is no entailment because it is the case that what is, logically, only contingently true may be guaranteed or endorsed (in
some way) by God so as to be epistemologically certain. (Such a
possibility may seem dubious at this stage in the discussion, but
something along these lines will be canvassed in the next chapter.)

[1] Locke, *Essay*, IV.10.6.

The sense of 'certain' here, as the sense of 'know' in proposition (c) above would differ both from Locke's strong view, which is reserved for analytic propositions and certain intuitions and what is deducible from these, and from Ayer's view in which what is known (besides analytic truths) – because it is not the only possibility compatible with the grounds alleged – is epistemologically corrigible. But Locke, taking the view that what can be *known* is very restricted, is committed to the view that those religious propositions that are not deducible from basic intuitions (as the existence of God is deducible), being only probably true, can only be believed.

It is true that Locke qualifies this in some remarks in his chapter 'Degrees of Assent'.[2] The qualification is quite formal, however. Discussing assent to testimony he writes:

'There is one sort of propositions that challenge the highest degree of our assent, upon bare testimony, whether the thing proposed agree or disagree with common experience and the ordinary course of things or no. The reason whereof is because the testimony is of such an one as cannot deceive nor be deceived, and that is of God himself. This carries with it assurance beyond doubt, evidence beyond exception. This is called by a peculiar name, *revelation*; and our assent to it, *faith*; which as absolutely determines our minds, and as perfectly excludes all wavering as our knowledge itself; and we may as well doubt of our own being as we can whether any revelation from God be true. So that faith is a settled and sure principle of assent and assurance, and leaves no manner of room for doubt or hesitation.'

This seems at first sight flatly to contradict the claims that faith is a case of probable belief. But the passage continues:

'Only we must be sure that it be divine revelation, and that we understand it right; else we shall expose ourselves to all the extravagancy of enthusiasm and all the error of wrong principles, if we have faith and assurance in what is not divine revelation.'

At first Locke seems to say that, besides the certain intuition we have of our own and God's existence, we can know (in this same strong sense) that certain propositions are revealed by God, because of the self-evidencing quality of these propositions. But Locke goes on to qualify this by setting up certain tests for purported revelations. The character of these tests is clearly seen in his two later chapters, 'Of Faith and Reason, and this Distinct Provinces' and 'Of Enthusiasm'.[3]

The thrust of the discussion in these chapters is anti-enthusiastic, for Locke is concerned to overthrow claims to religious knowledge that are based on personal inspiration and immediate revelation. Given that Locke believes that there are revealed propositions, and that there are those who lay claim to personal inspiration, the crucial question is how a revealed proposition is to be identified. In the *Essay* at least[4] Locke does not say 'It is a matter of faith that p is a revealed proposition', because this would be quite compatible with the enthusiastic claims that he dearly wished to rebut. That is, Locke distinguishes between 'p, a revealed proposition, is to be believed' and 'That p is a revealed proposition is a matter of faith'. The first of these is analytically true for Locke, though it might be thought from the remarks of his quoted above that it was no more than an important contingent truth. But it is analytically true for Locke and for all theists that, because God cannot deceive, if he reveals p, p must be true. The second proposition is rejected by Locke and he replaces it by one of the form 'p is warrantably believed to be a revealed proposition if and only if conditions a, b and c are met'. That is to say, for p to be regarded as a revealed proposition it must be possible to identify it as such logically independently of anyone's believing it to be such. The belief that it is revealed is based on the criteria of identification.

'For matter of faith being only divine revelation and nothing else, *faith*, as we use the word (called commonly, *divine faith*) has to do with no propositions but those which are supposed to be divinely revealed. So that I do not see how those who make revelation alone the sole object of *faith* can say that it is a matter of *faith*, and not of *reason*, to believe that such or such a proposition, to be found in such or such a book, is of divine

---

[3] Chapters 18 and 19.
[4] Locke does argue something like this in the course of his long controversy with Stillingfleet.

inspiration, unless it be revealed that that proposition, or all in that book, was communicated by divine inspiration.'⁵

'Whatever God hath revealed is certainly true : no doubt can be made of it. This is the proper object of *faith*; but whether it be a divine revelation or no, *reason* must judge, which can never permit the mind to reject a greater evidence to embrace what is less evident, nor allow it to entertain probability in opposition to knowledge and certainty.'⁶

Reason must judge whether or not p is a revelation. But on what grounds? At this point Locke introduces two separate problems, which we can call the problem of identification and the problem of meaning, respectively. Though Locke repeatedly makes the point that reason must first identify a proposition as revealed before it can be believed, he is not at all explicit on what the criteria of such propositions are. They seem to be striking events, such as miracles (for those who were originally inspired) and credible reports of these events for those living later who can only hear or read of them. Locke refers to these generally as matters 'extrinsical to the persuasions themselves'.⁷ Further, reason must indicate the meaning of the revelation. 'It still belongs to *reason* to judge of the truth of its being a revelation and of the signification of the words wherein it is delivered.'⁸

But whatever the exact grounds on which propositions are judged to form part of a revelation from God, and on which the meaning of such propositions is decided, the logical effect of insisting on such criteria is that they can be regarded only as contingently true, and, what is more to the point, only *believable*, not (in Locke's strong sense) *knowable*. That is to say, Locke seems to want to maintain the following three propositions :

(a) There are certain religious propositions the truth of which can be *known*. (In particular for Locke, the proposition 'God exists'.)

(b) What God reveals is certainly true. (Because God is not a deceiver, and whatever he asserts will not be a deception.)

(c) The ground for a proposition being revealed is (for example) its being accompanied by miracles. Hence revealed propositions can only be probably true because they are only

⁵ op. cit., IV.18.6. ⁶ Section 10.
⁷ op. cit., IV.19.14. ⁸ ibid., IV.18.8.

validated by a proposition (or a set of propositions) which is empirically true.

The second of these propositions is analytically true for Locke and for any theist, as was pointed out above. Yet for Locke no one can *know* that a particular proposition is revealed by God, he can only warrantably believe it, given appropriate evidence. By this he seems to mean that the function of reason is to present to the mind what is more evident in order that the mind may reject what is less evident. If there are two propositions p and q that are conclusions about matters of fact, and are inconsistent with each other, and there is less evidence for the truth of p than for q, then reason must reject p for q. Again, reason never allows the mind to entertain probability in opposition to knowledge and certainty. *'Nothing that is contrary to, and inconsistent with, the clear and self-evident dictates of reason has a right to be urged or assented to as a matter of faith, wherein reason hath nothing to do.'*[9] So what purports to be a revelation from God must not be inconsistent with our demonstrative and intuitive knowledge, nor with our beliefs about the world.[10] This second condition is more important for his views on religious belief.

So for a proposition to be a revelation it must be consistent with intuitive or demonstrative knowledge, and be probably true. But then Locke's dictum, quoted earlier, that 'Whatever God hath revealed is certainly true' cannot be understood as an epistemic claim. God's revelation is certain, but we can never know this, because, on Locke's own admission, no amount of empirical evidence will ever establish our right to *know* that a putative revealed proposition is a part of God's revelation. This applies even where the content of the putative revelation is a matter that is 'above reason', for it is still the case that reason must judge as to the credentials of that revelation, and as to the significance of the terms it employs.

In the chapter 'Of Enthusiasm' Locke argues against the possibility of new revelations. They are not disallowed *a priori*, but for them to be accepted into the stock of existing revealed propositions they must meet either of two conditions. They must conform 'to the principles of reason or to the word of God, which

---

[9] ibid., IV.18.19.
[10] See also ibid., IV.18.5.

is attested revelation'.[11] Attested revelation is just putative revelation supported by the appropriate signs or 'proofs'.

Thus we see the holy men of old, who had *revelations* from God, had something else besides that internal light of assurance in their own minds to testify to them that it was from God . . . had outward signs to convince them of the author of those revelations. And when they were to convince others, they had a power given them to justify the truth of their commission from heaven, and by visible signs to assert the divine authority of a message they were sent with.[12]

Locke gives the examples of Moses and the burning bush, and Gideon and the fleece, as examples of what he means.[13]

The appeal to miracles as validating conditions for revelation became part of the standard Protestant apologetic, even after Hume's treatment of the question. Yet even supposing that the appeal to miracles is in this way open to no serious objection, such evidence could never be evidence for knowledge, but only for belief, because the miracles, being contingent events in the past, are believed to have happened, not known to have happened. On the basis of prophecy and miracle no one is ever entitled, in Locke's view, to say 'I know that p is a revealed truth' only 'I believe, or am assured, that this is a revealed truth'. But if this is so, how can Locke possibly think that it provides an adequate epistemological structure for an infallible revelation? Using miracle and prophecy as rational supports only succeeds in pushing the crucial epistemological questions one stage further back. The questions now become, How is one to know that a particular event is an act of God? and, How is one to know (in Locke's sense) that it has happened? To the second question Locke's answer has to be that one never can. To appeal, in answer to the first question, to miracle and prophecy is an obvious *petitio*.

What Locke's views amount to, therefore, is that claims for the *revealed* character of any proposition cannot be isolated from other claims to knowledge. What God reveals is infallibly true (by

---

[11] ibid., IV.19.15.   [12] ibid., IV.19.15.

[13] In his discussion of Locke, F. Copleston is surely mistaken when he says that Locke does not embark on 'the question where the revelation is to be found and through what particular organs it has been made'. (*History of Philosophy*, vol. IV, p. 122).

definition), yet such infallible truths can never be identified with certainty, only with probability. But 'It is probable that p is infallibly true' entails 'It is probable that p is true' which in turn is equivalent to 'p is probably true'.

On this view revelation becomes secularized in the sense that a claim to know something by revelation is a conjecture that is for ever open to refutation. Not that it is logically refutable only, but it is epistemologically refutable, also, in just the same way as conjectures in other fields of enquiry. Religious claims are critical, not dogmatic. The religious significance or authority of a proposition is only contingently related to its meaning. This is the consequence of Locke's belief in the need of criteria to ward off enthusiasm, and his rejection of any appeal to the self-validating character of religious language. By implication he would reject both what was referred to earlier as the 'strict autonomy' view of religious language, the thesis that the criteria of meaningfulness are internal to religion, and the 'weak autonomy' view, the thesis that religion, and hence religious language, serves distinctive needs.

II

The Lockean analysis of religious belief that we have sketched forms an important element in the religious apologetic of Butler's *Analogy of Religion*. For Butler the proposition 'There will be a future life' is not to be understood as 'It is known that there will be a future life' or 'It is certain that there will be a future life' but as 'A future life is more likely and hence more credible than not'. The credibility of a future life, and of other distinctive religious claims, is rooted for Butler in certain natural analogies. Thus :

'Particular analogies do most sensibly show us, that there is nothing to be thought strange, in our being to exist in another state of life. And that we are now living beings, affords a strong probability that we shall *continue* so; unless there be some positive ground, and there is none from reason or analogy, to think death will destroy us . . . The supposition then, which in all reason we are to go upon, is, that our living nature will *continue* after death.'[14]

[14] Vol. 1 of Butler's *Works*, ed. Gladstone (1897), p. 147.

Examining this argument would not be to the point here. Butler grants that such an argument is not theoretically satisfactory – that is to say, a future life cannot be demonstrated. But the argument from the analogy of nature provides sufficient grounds for the belief to be practically effective. It 'serves the purposes of religion'. By this last phrase Butler seems to mean that, if it is the case that it is more probable that there will be a future life than that there will not be, this provides support for living religiously, which for Butler means living morally, because of the prospect of future rewards and punishments. Someone who thinks that it is highly likely that there will be a future life of rewards and punishments will behave in just the same way as if it could, *per impossible*, be demonstrated that there is to be a future life. The use of such analogies is thus to 'remove presumptions' against important religious doctrines, and hence at the practical level to provide motives for right living.

'20 *Ask, not, does it satisfy? but, does
it bind to action?*

One might add farther; that whether the motives or the evidence for any course of action be satisfactory, meaning here, by that word, what satisfies a man, that such a course of action will in event be for his good; this need never be, and I think, strictly speaking, never is, the practical question in common matters. But the practical question in all cases is, Whether the evidence for a course of action be such, as, taking in all circumstances, makes the faculty within us, which is the guide and judge of conduct, determine that course of action to be prudent. Indeed, satisfaction that it will be for our interest or happiness, abundantly determines an action to be prudent : but evidence almost infinitely lower than this, determines actions to be so too; even in the conduct of every day.'[15]

The question of survival after death is not the only religious doctrine treated in this way. In discussing what he refers to as 'scripture-history', Butler maintains that it is 'to be admitted as an authentic genuine history, till somewhat positive be alleged sufficient to invalidate it.'[16] That is, 'scripture-history', as the

[15] ibid., pp. 298–9.   [16] ibid., p. 251.

phrase implies, is simply a set of historical hypotheses, and the onus is firmly on those who wish to disprove particular events to show that the Bible makes false empirical claims. And Butler goes on to illustrate at length the features of the Bible that make it credible as history.

I. T. Ramsey is only partly right in the account of Butler's views he gives in *Religious Language*.[17] He is correct in maintaining that it is not an implication of Butler's view that religious belief is detached and half-hearted. Butler's stress is on the fact that, for all practical purposes, belief is a matter of certainty, granted that the belief is well-grounded. But it is a different question whether Butler's view involves what Ramsey calls a 'total commitment' – 'a commitment which sees in a situation all that the understanding can give us and more'. Butler's view does not involve him in going beyond 'rational considerations', rather the reverse. Religion, for Butler, is a case of the sort of belief that informs day-to-day living. The 'rational considerations' that belief goes beyond (assuming that this is an acceptable way of putting the point) are not matters of speculation but those matters that we can be absolutely certain of. What is distinctive about religious beliefs is that they are about religious matters. It is the content of such beliefs that gives them their importance. Similarly when Butler says, in the Conclusion of Part I of the *Analogy*, that it is false that 'gross bodies are ourselves' (i.e. when he argues that materialism is false), the grounds he has for making this assertion are not, as Ramsey thinks, a 'discernment' but *evidence*. Materialism is 'contrary to experience', so Butler thinks. It is not therefore a case of a situation that is 'spatio-temporal and more'. Rather it is that which is spatio-temporal, our experience of ourselves, that for Butler probabilifies the 'more', immortality and a future of rewards or punishments.

Butler's stance is that of an anti-sceptic who takes for granted the empiricist claim that there can be no theoretical certainty about contingent matters of fact. The possibility of a future life is one such contingent proposition, but scepticism about it can be mitigated (so Butler thinks) by appeal to the analogies of nature. Those who are sceptical about future life are asking for a degree of validation that is in the nature of things impossible. But, by analogy from the processes of nature, it can be shown that it is more likely than not that life will continue after death, or that the disciples were not duped about the character of Jesus, and this is all that religion, a practical matter of living virtuously, requires.

The whole argument from the analogies of nature gets what force it has from the assumption that religion is a 'common matter', concerned with the interest and happiness of men, and that it must be regulated according to the usual rules of prudence. Religious belief is not primarily cognitive, but practical; regulative, though in a different sense from the way in which Kant thought of religious belief as regulative. Religious belief is continuous with our beliefs about ordinary matters of fact. These are handled on prudential grounds. What makes an ordinary matter of fact important to someone is that he might lose money by it, or cause unpleasantness to himself or to others (or conversely gain financially, or become happier). In an analogous way, what makes religion important, and what gives religious doctrines their practical force, is that it is highly likely that there will be an after-life in which virtue will be rewarded and vice punished. People do business, plan, marry on less than certainty, so why not in religion?

The explicit connection between religion and prudence is even more striking in the case of William Paley. In his *Moral and Political Philosphy* (1785) virtue is defined as 'the doing good to mankind, in obedience to the will of God, for the sake of everlasting happiness'.[18] Virtue and prudence are identified in everything but their scope; virtue is 'religiously-informed prudence' where 'religiously-informed' means 'based on a belief in future rewards and punishments':

'To us there are two great questions: I. Will there be after this life any distribution of rewards and punishments at all? II. If there be, what actions will be rewarded, and what will be punished? The first question comprises the credibility of the Christian religion, together with the presumptive proofs of a

[18] *Works*, ed. E. Paley (1830), vol. 3, p. 28.

future retribution from the light of nature. The second question comprises the province of morality.'[19]

The reasons for thinking that religion is to our advantage are not conclusive. We may be deceived, just as the disciples of Jesus may have been, but it is not likely. For while the reasons for religion are not conclusive, they are sufficient to make it wise to practise religion, and to be happy under the government of the Author of nature. And in the same way that the addition of probabilities increase the likelihood of a particular event, so 'the truth of our religion, like the truth of common matters, is to be judged by all the evidence taken together'.[20]

The purpose of this sketch of the views of Locke and Butler on religious belief is to provide material for the construction of a model of religious belief which corresponds in fact more or less closely to the view of belief held by the dominant tradition of apologists in England – Butler, Paley, and a host of minor figures. Put schematically the view can be understood as follows : A religiously believes p if and only if

(a) p is a proposition having a certain content e.g. about the character of God, or the life of Jesus, or life after death, or prayer.

(b) p has evidence to support it, drawn either from history or from natural analogies, which makes it more likely to be true than to be false.

(c) Believing p to be true on the grounds outlined in (b) has a practical religious effect, to promote a life of virtue and piety. Each of these conditions (a) – (c) seems necessary, and jointly sufficient, for this model of religious belief. It may be that (c) is not the effect of (b) so much as a feature of (b).

'Being religious' is understood, on this view, as being a matter of behaving in certain ways, from motives that are prudential. The relation between such actions and the religious beliefs that support them is clearly contingent. A person could (in this sense) be religious for other reasons than those that he actually has; he could refrain from stealing for other prudential reasons than that he believes in an after-life of rewards and punishments. Beliefs with a religious meaning enter only contingently into religion in this sense, which is primarily a matter of acting in

---

[19] ibid., pp. 42–3.   [20] Butler, op. cit., p. 287.

certain ways, rather than in believing certain articles of faith. The idea of 'natural religion' is not far from the surface.

Though, as we saw, this view is 'regulative' and 'practical' in the sense that the propositions believed provide motives for action, the propositions are cognitive in character. It is because they are cognitive, and probable, that they have the religious import they do have. That is to say, this view of religious propositions as regulative is to be distinguished from the Kantian view in which it is denied that religious utterances are cognitive. Further, religious beliefs are regulative in the sense outlined only if a particular view of morals is presupposed, in which morality and prudence are virtually indistinguishable. The propositions of religion have the force they do have because they provide motives for prudent living. For someone who rejects such a morality the belief in an after life of punishments and rewards will have no moral appeal.

Since a proposition, in order to be a religious belief, has to have evidence it follows that certain religious propositions at least are corrigible, hence falsifiable. Not all, for it must be borne in mind that for Locke at least the existence of God was a matter of knowledge, not belief. It was not corrigible. But for later apologists in this tradition even this changed when the argument from design was used as a theistic proof. Excepting the proposition 'God exists' (in the case of Locke), falsifiability was not only a feature of religious beliefs, it was also a *necessary* feature, given their epistemological status. It follows in turn that religious beliefs are revisable in principle, though a certain immunity to revision in practice is purchased by grounding them in the analogies of nature as Butler did. But on this view the religious man believes in, say, the figure of Christ given in the Bible to the extent to which the claims made there tally with, or at least do not go against, secular historical findings.

It was pointed out earlier that one reason why the term 'belief' is appropriate for religious belief is that on some views religious belief involves accepting testimony, and so involves taking someone's (or some document's) word for what is believed. Belief, that is, is used not only in contrast with knowledge but also in contrast with getting to know something at first hand, for oneself. Religious belief is also assent to testimony, in Locke's

words 'assent to any proposition . . . upon the credit of the proposer as coming from God, in some extraordinary way of communication'.[21] Locke's view implies (what he elsewhere claims
explicitly) that it is impossible for a person to know and believe
the same proposition at the same time. He maintains this because he ties knowledge to one source (intuition, deduction),
and belief to another (sense-experience, testimony). Yet it is
possible for an individual to believe what another knows (e.g.
that the angles of a triangle add up to two right angles), where
he is told this. And it is in terms of this idea that Locke at times
regards religious belief. It is a person's belief that p on the testimony of another who has received this from God. But, as we
saw, this involves Locke in discussing the criteria of a revelation
and adopting an essentially rationalistic position on the question.

   Finally, it seems from some of the things Locke says that
religious belief is 'propositional' in the rather restricted sense that
what is believed are assertions from God. That is to say, revelation is simply a making known of a series of facts that would not
otherwise be known. The propositions are declarations by God.
This does not seem to be a necessary feature of the model of
belief under discussion, yet it is worth noticing. Thus he says
that 'Faith be founded on the testimony of God . . . revealing any
proposition to us'[22] and '*Revelation* is natural *reason* enlarged
by a new set of discoveries communicated by God immediately'.[23]
Locke does not appear to think of revelation as containing other
than propositions having the force of assertions – no commands,
or promises, for example. Revelation is simply the 'discovery of
truths', those truths 'that are beyond the discovery of our natural
faculties and above *reason*'. Thus, that part of the angels rebelled
against God and thereby lost their first happy state, and that
the dead shall rise and live again.'[24]

III

By altering the second of the set of necessary and sufficient conditions of this model of belief, as outlined earlier, a different
notion of belief is obtained, though one that has interesting

---

[21] *Essay*, IV.18.2.   [22] ibid., IV.18.5.
[23] ibid., IV.19.4.   [24] ibid., IV.18.7.

affinities to the Locke-Butler view just discussed. That is, if belief is regarded not as what is probably the case, but what is possibly the case, not as a case of prudence but of risk, this amounts to something like the view of F. R. Tennant.

In Tennant's view belief and faith are closely connected, and while it is belief that concerns us in this study something must be said about how Tennant regards this connection. Religious faith is a species of that faith that is present, he thinks, in every human enquiry, particularly in science. Religious faith is a venture, but then all intellectual activities presuppose such a venture. The rational justification for such venturing is pragmatic. It is characteristic of faith, whether religious or secular, that it goes beyond the data in supposing certain things to be the case. This supposition either is or is not justified in subsequent practice. Newton's hypotheses about motion, and Columbus's view about land to the west of Spain, are cases of faith.

'Belief is more or less constrained by fact or Actuality that already is or will be, independently of any striving of ours, and which convinces us. Faith, on the other hand, reaches beyond the Actual or the given to the ideally possible, which in the first instance it creates, as the mathematician posits his entities, and then by practical activity may realise or bring into Actuality.'[25]

The scientist's belief in induction is a case of a faith-venture, according to Tennant.[26] This is difficult to accept. A scientist's belief in induction is heuristic, a presupposition of his doing any science at all. It is hard to see what there is about this that could fairly be called a 'faith-venture'. No doubt there are scientific 'ventures' – hypotheses – but the belief in induction is not one of them.

The second point that Tennant makes, after the point that all intellectual activity requires faith, is that the venture is determined by human interest and so is not 'mere prudence of probability'.

'It involves the determination, once it has gathered content, to be guided by such experience as we have, rather than by none at all; it equally involves the determination, before its Actual content has been secured, to venture into the realm of the possible and the ideal, and to experiment there.'[27]

[25] *Philosophical Theology*, vol. 1 (1928), p. 297.
[26] ibid., p. 298.   [27] ibid., p. 299.

By 'venture', then, Tennant does not mean a hunch or a shot in the dark; faith as venture is guided by 'such experience as we have' yet it is not proportioned to the evidence in the sort of way advocated by Locke and Butler. Religious belief is not therefore just a well-grounded inductive generalization, it is 'fallible clairvoyance'. Because, in Tennant's view, faith (in this sense) underlies every acquisition of knowledge or 'so-called knowledge', *religious* faith is not peculiarly irrational.

'The theistic interpretation of the world is but a carrying to completion, and an explication, of the implicit belief of science in what is vaguely called the rationality of the world.'[28]

Though it differs in important respects from the Locke-Butler view, both models have interesting elements in common. Religious belief, in both cases, is in a *formally* similar position to general empirical beliefs, including scientific beliefs. But whereas for Locke and Butler religious belief stands to knowledge as probability stands to certainty, for Tennant the 'faith principle' underlies all rational activities. Where for Butler the acquisition of knowledge consists in the accumulation of evidence, and religious belief, to be acceptable, has to be consistent with this body of evidence, and can never be 'disproportioned' to it, for Tennant science consists in the propounding and testing of hypotheses, and religious belief consists in the propounding of hypotheses at the point where science leaves off.

In both cases the contrast is made between religious belief, and certainty or knowledge. For the earlier view religious belief can only be belief, while for Tennant 'so-called' scientific knowledge is in fact only a set of pragmatically justifiable hypotheses. Religious belief, like a tested scientific hypothesis, is a case of certitude, not certainty. That is, the evidence (at best) warrants belief and a feeling of certainty or assurance that what is believed is true. It does not entail the truth of what is believed. And whereas Tennant's thesis about religious belief appears at first sight to be sheer irrationalism, it is in his view an instance of that which underlies all rational activity. Despite important differences, for all three – Locke, Butler and Tennant – religious belief is secular, corrigible and pragmatic.

[28] ibid., p. 300.

6

SELF-AUTHENTICATION

In contrast to the view outlined in the previous chapter in which religious belief is based on probability, it is possible to offer an account of belief in terms of the reception of a religious authority, in which what is believed is regarded by the believer not as probable but as certain. A view such as this was foreshadowed in the general discussion of knowledge and certainty in Chapter 4. This view will now be set out at some length, using mainly two sources from Protestant Reformed theological discussion, the writings of John Calvin and John Owen. The discussion will be in three parts – a consideration of the sense in which 'belief' is used; the meaning of 'self-authentication'; and finally the sense in which such beliefs may be regarded as certain. The purpose of this, as the other models, is to illustrate the main thesis of the book. The merits or demerits of the individual views are not here at issue.

I

To say that religious belief is assent to testimony is not very illuminating by itself. For assent is compatible with a whole range of responses which are in turn incompatible with religious belief. Thus one can assent to a decision, a plan, or an imperative : one can assent half-heartedly, or guardedly, or unhesitatingly. For religious belief to involve assent it must involve it *in some sense*, with unqualified assent perhaps, or with the sort of assent that gives rise to trust.[1] In what follows 'assent' is used with the following entailment : that if A assents to p he regards p as true – 'assent' and 'accept' will be used interchangeably.

Calvin stresses the fact that faith involves personal commitment and trust, and also the fact that faith involves belief in

[1] On the need to make such qualifications see Kevin Presa 'Assent, belief and faith', *Sophia* (October 1968).

certain propositions, and that it is distinct from what he calls 'comprehension'. His definition of faith is

'A firm and certain knowledge of God's benevolence toward us, founded upon the truth of the freely given promise in Christ, both revealed to our minds and sealed upon our hearts through the Holy Spirit.'[2]

The object of belief is God's promise, that is, a particular proposition or set of propositions. And while faith is certain (an important point to be discussed later in this chapter), and while Calvin calls what the promise gives 'knowledge', the information that the believer is given is not the same as that received though sense-experience alone.

'When we call faith "knowledge" we do not mean comprehension of the sort that is commonly concerned with those things which fall under human sense perception.

'Those things which we know through faith are nonetheless absent from us and go unseen. From this we conclude that the knowledge of faith consists in assurance rather than in comprehension.'[3]

What is believed is, to use a contrast that will be examined in Chapter 8, a case of knowledge by description rather than knowledge by acquaintance, and Calvin calls it knowledge because of its certainty, not because it is something that the believer can get to know for himself, by perception, for example.

This distinction between faith and comprehension is a familiar scholastic one: the difference betwen Aquinas and Calvin on this point is merely terminological. Calvin calls knowledge and faith what Thomas calls faith, but both distinguish this concept from knowledge in the sense of sense-experience, and both (Aquinas explicitly and Calvin implicitly by his insistence on the certainty of faith) distinguish it from opinion.[4]

---

[2] *Institutes of the Christian Religion*, trans. F. L. Battles, 1960, III.2.7.
[3] ibid., III.2.14.
[4] Calvin's epistemology is a matter of widespread debate. See e.g. E. A. Dowey, *The Knowledge of God in Calvin's Theology* (1952), T. H. L. Parker, *The Doctrine of the Knowledge of God: A Study in Calvin's Theology* (Second Edition, 1969), B. B. Warfield, 'Calvin's Doctrine of the Knowledge of God', in *Calvin and Calvinism* (1931).

In both Aquinas and Calvin the denial that the knowledge that the believer can have of God is comprehensive is connected with the claim that it is impossible to know the essence of God and that therefore God is to be known only by his effects. The awareness of these effects can demonstrate that God exists (Aquinas tries to show this in the Five Ways), even though such demonstrations cannot help us to know God comprehensively. In Calvin there is little, if any, stress on the effects of God's activity providing premises for a demonstration of his existence, for though he allows that 'upon his individual works he has engraved unmistakable marks of his glory' he goes on to claim that men reject this evidence.[5] He is as insistent as Aquinas is that God is incomprehensible. Calvin's characteristic way of putting this is to deny that God is revealed (either naturally or in Scripture) 'as he is in himself' but as related in some way to his creation, as Creator or Redeemer. It is in such terms that Calvin would meet difficulties about identifying God.[6] It is folly, he would say, to attempt to refer to God 'as he is in himself'; reference must be made via his 'effects' in nature and history. The claim of Aquinas and Calvin that men can have knowledge, though not comprehensive knowledge, of God has implications for their views about theological language. In Aquinas this is developed in terms of a theory of analogy, while Calvin, though his views are less worked out than those of Aquinas on this topic, stresses that God 'accommodates' himself to the understanding of men.

'For who even of slight intelligence does not understand that, as nurses commonly do with infants, God is wont in a measure to 'lisp' in speaking to us? Thus such forms of speaking do not so much express clearly what God is like as to accommodate the knowledge of him to our slight capacity.'[7]

[5] This touches on the thorny question of the extent to which Calvin presupposes a natural theology in the developing argument of the *Institutes*. Warfield (op. cit.) maintains that he does.

[6] *Institutes*, I.4.1., I.5.9.

[7] ibid., I.13.1.

II

The close connection between faith and testimony has already been noted. The object of religious belief for Protestants such as Calvin is the Bible regarded as a 'self-authenticating' divine revelation. The reasons for believing the message of the Bible are not ecclesiastical – the testimony of the Church; or historical – that there is more evidence to support the truth of the Bible than its falsity; but they are reasons that are internal to the teaching of the Bible. The idea of self-authentication is a difficult one to get clear.

The view can be set out most satisfactorily by dismissing a series of alternatives. It is not that when someone reads a self-authenticating document he can never mistake its meaning or its meaningfulness. Those Reformed theologians who use the notion of self-authentication, such as Calvin and John Owen (1616–1683),[8] are not saying that if A reads the Bible he can no more doubt that it is God's word than he can doubt, when he has a certain sensation, that he has that sensation. 'Self-authentic' is not another term for 'incorrigible' as this has been used in debates about phenomenalism, for example. What Calvin and Owen do say is, however, rather similar. Those who come to accept the Bible as a self-authenticating divine revelation are as convinced of its truth as someone who has a sensation of sweetness is convinced of its sweetness.

'As to their question – How can we be assured this has sprung from God unless we have recourse to the decree of the church? – it is as if someone asked: Whence will we learn to distinguish light from darkness, white from black, sweet from bitter? Indeed, Scripture exhibits fully as clear evidence of its own truth as

[8] Owen was a leading Puritan theologian and Vice-Chancellor of Oxford University, 1652–60. The notion of self-authentication used in several of his writings was not peculiar to Owen but is a fundamental feature of Reformed theology. (See, for example, *The Westminster Confession of Faith*, ch. 1 and the catena of quotations from Reformed theologians in B. B. Warfield's article, 'The Westminster Doctrine of Holy Scripture', in *The Westminster Assembly and its Work* (1931).

white and black things do of their colour, or sweet and bitter things do of their taste.'[9]

Further, this notion of self-authentication is not the same as that employed in many modern religious discussions, in which it is said to be a criterion of 'meeting' or 'encountering' God that the experience is self-authenticating, that 'it shines by its own light independently of the abstract reflections of philosophy'. This modern notion seems to be open to several objections, notably that such a claim as 'I encountered God in Christ' is not a report of an immediate experience, but of an interpreted experience, and that such an experience cannot have existential import without being corrigible, which regarding it as 'self-authenticating' seems to rule out.

The view that we have attributed to Calvin and Owen seems to differ from this modern view in at least one important respect. What is said to be self-authenticating is identifiable independently of the experience of self-authentication. 'Self-authentic' is a property not of an experience but of a proposition or set of propositions. Hence it is theoretically possible to overthrow the claim that such a proposition is self-authenticating, and overthrow would actually take place if the claims made by the proposition – for instance, the claim to meet certain needs – were unfulfilled.

One consequence of the truth of a given claim is that it would hold good for anyone accepting it. If Johnny's uncle says 'If you're a good boy I'll take you on the Big Dipper', this promise is shown to be true (or, if some object to the idea of a promise being true, the proposition that it embodies – 'Johnny will be taken to the Big Dipper if he is a good boy' – will be shown to be true), if Johnny puts his uncle to the test, is good, and ends up on the Big Dipper. Calvin and Owen would say that this is how it is in the case of the Bible, though they would add that only those will put the promises to the test who have certain needs or beliefs, i.e. to whom the promises are meaningful. They are not saying that 'p is true' *means* 'p has certain effects or

[9] *Institutes*, I.7.2. Compare John Owen, *The Reason of Faith; or, An Answer Unto That Inquiry, 'Wherefore we believe the Scripture to be the Word of God'* (1677), reprinted in *Works*, ed. W. Goold (1850–3), vol. 4, p. 64.

consequences', but that if p is true it will have certain effects. 'God promises forgiveness' is true if, and only if, it is the case that God promises forgiveness. If it is true, then certain effects can be expected to follow; for example, that men who ask for forgiveness will be forgiven.

There is a further sense in which the propositions said to be self-authenticating are testable; the historical claims that provide some of the necessary conditions for some of the assertions, or promises, in the Bible are, as all historical events are, corrigible. But such falsifiability is for Owen of secondary importance.

It is in the arousal and satisfaction of certain distinctive beliefs, hopes and fears that the character of the Bible as God's word is discerned. God authenticates himself to men in Scripture and enables them to discern this fact by arousing and satisfying certain distinctive needs as they read it. This arousal of distinctive needs is what Calvin refers to as the 'internal testimony of the Holy Spirit'.

'Distinctive' here is a strong expression. It is not simply that the needs are distinctive in the way in which the need for food is distinct from the need for water, say, but that the needs are *identified as* the needs they are taken to be *only* by means of the self-authenticated revelation. A man might say 'I believe myself to be in need of divine forgiveness'; this is a religiously genuine need if, and only if, the notion for forgiveness here is that employed in the document. Not every need is a need for forgiveness, and not every need for forgiveness is a need for forgiveness in the appropriate *sense* of 'forgiveness'. Conversely, no longer to believe in the need for divine forgiveness is no longer to identify one's needs by reference to the claims of the document. At that point the document ceases to be authenticated.

To understand fully the significance (i.e. the point or meaningfulness) of the locutions of the Bible it is necessary to become 'engaged', so that certain promises in the Bible are understood not merely as reports of promises to certain individuals in history, but as promises to the reader. They will not be seen as such unless they are regarded as being relevant, and one kind of necessary condition of relevance is the belief that one has certain needs. Thus a promise of forgiveness will not be regarded by the reader as a promise to him unless he believes he needs forgiving. Further, regarding the locutions as meaningful, and hence as relevant in this way, provides the only warrant needed for believing the propositions concerned, whereas in the case of propositions that are not self-authenticating, authentication has to be through other sets of propositions, or through observation

This is not simply that the locutions are believed to be true because they are helpful. Rather it is as considered as being true, (truth from God), that they are believed, and it is in their reception as true that their power to arouse and satisfy distinctive religious needs consists.[10] It is because they are presented as true that there is a *prima facie* obligation on the part of the believer to rebut charges that the locutions are meaningless or false. There would be no such obligation if they were regarded simply as helpful aids. But the authority of the locutions does not rest in the grounds on which objections to them are met.[11]

It is difficult to say whether this fairly represents what Protestant theologians mean by the self-authenticating 'power' of the Bible, but it is offered as a plausible account of what they might mean. It is beyond doubt that they wish to make a firm distinction between those reasons for believing that are independent of the authority's teaching, and those that are part of it. John Owen puts this distinction in terms of a contrast between *external* and *internal* reasons for believing. By external reasons or arguments Owen means such arguments as the fact that the Bible was an ancient book, wonderfully preserved, coherent and so on. But such considerations provide only a moral assurance of the truth of the Bible, that is 'the arguments and motives used, though strong, are *human* and *fallible*, and, therefore, the conclusion we make from them is so also, and wherein we may be deceived'.[12] That is, if these arguments are thought of in terms of the contrast between the Butler view of religious belief, and

---

[10] This insistence on the *truth* of the self-authenticating revelation, coupled with the place found for 'external' reasons (see below) sharply distinguishes the Reformed view from S. T. Coleridge's.

[11] Diogenes Allen, *The Reasonableness of Faith* (1968), has been of considerable help in rationally reconstructing what Owen says about self-authentication and the internal testimony of the Holy Spirit, though Professor Allen may not approve of the use to which his ideas have been put.

[12] *The Reason of Faith, Works* IV, p. 46. *The Westminster Confession of Faith* (1647) has a similar contrast between external and internal reasons (I.5).

Owen's own view, they support the Butler position. And though the belief they warrant, that the Bible is God's Word, is for Owen a true belief, it is not a case of *religious* belief.

'Now, these arguments are all human and fallible. Exalt them unto the greatest esteem possible, yet because they are not demonstrations, nor do necessarily beget a certain knowledge in us (which, indeed, if they did, there were no room left for faith or our obedience therein), they produce an opinion only, though in the highest kind of probability, and firm against objections: for we will allow the utmost assurance that can be claimed upon them. But this is exclusive of all divine faith, as to any article, thing, matter or object to be believed.'[13]

Owen contrasts the certainty that is the product of external with that which is the product of internal reasons. But what is the evidence for the certainty of faith? The standard Protestant answer before the deism and rationalism of the eighteenth century was that the Bible was its own testimony.

Epistemologically, this amounts to an appeal to intuition, or what Owen called 'illumination'. When illuminated, the believer 'is enabled to discern the evidences of the divine original and authority of the Scripture that are in itself, as well as assent unto the truth contained in it'.[14] He is careful to distinguish this intuitionism from a religious enthusiasm which appeals to 'external immediate revelations', just as ready as Locke was to oppose 'enthusiasm' in the *Essay*. The illumination

'is an internal revelation of that which is outward and antecedent unto it; beyond the bounds thereof it is not to be extended. And if any pretend unto *immediate revelations* of things not before revealed, we have no concernment in their pretences.'[15]

This intuition or illumination is not the grounds for the believer believing what he does. It is the means or 'power' by which what is present in the Bible is believed.

This divine testimony, the Bible in the case of orthodox Protestant theologians such as Calvin and Owen, is not to be thought

[13] ibid., p. 50.
[14] ibid., p. 57.
[15] ibid., p. 59.

SELF-AUTHENTICATION 109

of as just another piece of probabilifying evidence for the truth
of certain religious propositions, but as epistemologically distinct
from such evidence. The character of this intuition requires some
explanation.

In discussing the foundations of knowledge A. M. Quinton
has distinguished between three different senses of intuition,[16]
and it is useful to think of Owen's position in the light of them.
They are : (a) A capacity to form correct beliefs in the absence
of the sort of evidence usually required to justify them. (b) A
Belief for which no reason can be given for accepting it. (c)
Logically intuitive beliefs, that is, beliefs which do not require
other beliefs to support them or to make them worthy of
acceptance.

If, as has been suggested, appeal to divine testimony is for
Calvin and Owen epistemologically distinct from other kinds of
evidence, then the third sense of 'intuition' must be what Owen
had in mind. The first sense is clearly irrelevant. Owen is not
saying that the believer 'just knows' and cannot say why. The
second is ruled out because, as has been shown, Owen has much
to say about reasons, both 'internal' and 'external'. To take the
third alternative, and say that by 'illumination' Owen meant the
possession of some logically intuitive belief, must be qualified in
two ways, however. As we noted earlier he did not say that the
possession of such intuitions was a universal or necessary feature
of the human mind, but stressed that it was dependent on divine
grace. Further, and connected with this, the certainty of such
propositions known by intuition was not due to 'natural light',
as it is in Cartesianism. Finally Owen would reject the idea that
the propositions of a self-authenticating document were analytic
truths, for he sharply distinguishes between the knowledge of
analytic propositions and the knowledge of revealed propositions.

Yet Owen would not, it seems, allow for the possibility of belief
in the propositions of revelation being well-grounded but false.
For this reason he is not faced with the Gettier counter-examples
noted earlier.

The certainty that Owen attributes to the propositions of
divine revelation raises a possible objection. G. E. Moore says,

[16] In *British Analytical Philosophy*, ed Bernard Williams and Alan Monte-
fiore (1961), p. 59.

in his paper 'Certainty', of certain material-object statements, that 'if *they* were not certain, then no proposition which implies the existence of anything external to the mind of the person who makes it is ever certain'.[17] Owen wishes to say that the truths of revelation are certain, and that men can know they are, by coming to appreciate their self-evidencing power. That is, in religion it is possible to know that p is certain, and not just, as with Butler, believe that it is. For Butler, as for empiricists in general, there is the problem about knowing that one knows, for the grounds which justify a belief never entail its truth.

Owen's position raises the following problem : on what grounds can Owen be sure that he has the Bible in front of him? If the grounds are only probable, the supposed self-authenticating authority, certain propositions of the Bible, are only probable, whatever Owen may say to the contrary. It is clear that he must take a position like Moore's if he is to avoid this objection.

Owen insists that statable reasons are not *required* to support the authority of the revelation. But this is not to say that such reasons are not *available*. The 'external' grounds already mentioned belong in this category. If the intuition is correct, then the internal evidence, the propositions of revelation, can be expected to coincide with or cohere with the external evidence, though it might be hard to show such coincidence in fact. Apologetics, on this view, would consist in the provision of such grounds where they are available. But lack of them does not invalidate the intuition. The primary validation of the religious authority is not dependent on the findings of secular history, but this is not to say that secondary validation is not so dependent.

Owen's general epistemology might be put as follows. There are analytic truths which the mind 'sees' to be the case, e.g. that the whole is greater than the part. Secondly, there are matters that are 'externally proposed to us'. By the use of the intellect a man is able to assent with different degrees of certainty according to the evidence he has. Of some things he has knowledge, of others only opinions. Finally there is faith (or belief) :

'This respects that power of our minds whereby we are able to assent unto any thing as true which we have no first principles

---

[17] G. E. Moore, *Philosophical Papers* (Collier Books Editions, 1962), p. 239.

concerning, no inbred notions of, nor can from more known principles make unto ourselves any certain rational conclusions concerning them. This is our assent *upon testimony*, whereon we believe many things which no sense, inbred principles, nor reasonings of our own, could either give us an acquaintance with or an assurance of. And this *assent* also hath not only *various degrees*, but it is also of *divers kinds*, according as the *testimony* is which it ariseth from and resteth on; as being *human* if that be *human*, and *divine* if that be so also.'[18]

So religious faith is a species of belief on testimony, in which the testimony is self-authenticating.

Coming to believe in the testimony of God revealed in the Bible is like becoming aware of a complicated *gestalt*. It is not like assenting to an analytic truth,[19] nor is the intuition, in Moore's terms, a non-natural property, but it is an awareness of the point of meaningfulness of certain propositions. Having the intuition consists in having a *'spiritual sense* of the *power and reality of the things believed'*.[20] He lists these 'divine characters'[21] and claims that

'there are on every *individual book of the Scripture*, particularly those named, those divine characters and *criteria* which are sufficient to difference them from all other writings whatever, and to testify their divine authority unto the minds and consciences of believers.'[22]

That is, the Bible has characteristics C which provide adequate evidence to the believer that it is God's word. But this adequate evidence, though necessary, is not a sufficient condition for anyone to believe that the Bible is God's word. It is also necessary that the reader of the Bible be in a certain condition. There are preconditions for accepting the Bible as God's word just as there are preconditions for a man taking what he sees to be a trout in a stream. So the fact that all people do not agree in their intuitions is not a valid objection against this position. Owen is quite prepared for this objection, and responds by putting

---

[18] Owen, op. cit., p. 83. [19] ibid., p. 88.
[20] ibid., p. 64. [21] ibid., pp. 94ff.
[22] ibid., p. 107.

different intuitions down to the 'natural blindness and darkness' of men's minds, and to the effects of training and education.[23]

III

What is distinctive about this view of religious belief is that the proposition believed is certainly true, and that the believer is certain that it is certainly true. That is, if p is religiously believed, p could not be more certain than it is (because it is the truth of God), though it could be known better. For example, unclarities in the conceptual content of the proposition could be removed, and more of its implications traced out. This view does recognize, however, that religious belief has degrees, and that sometimes a believer doubts. The statements made above are, therefore, to be taken to be about full-formed religious belief.

But just how is this notion of certainty to be taken? Owen does not use 'belief' in contrast to 'knowledge' when expounding his view because of its 'parenthetical' character. He is clear that authentic religious belief entails the truth of what is believed. 'Belief' is used, among other reasons, because 'knowledge' is reserved for truths known 'comprehensively'. As was shown earlier 'p is certainly true' can be understood in several different ways: as 'p is analytically true' or 'A feels certain as to p' or 'p is morally certain'.

But when, on this model, religious beliefs are regarded as certain, something distinct from any of these senses of 'certain' is meant. A number of things makes this clear. For one thing, the propositions of faith are regarded as informative and not simply about the meanings of words. For example, the statement 'Christ died on the cross to reconcile men to God' is certain (for them) but not because it is a tautology as 'Christ who died on the cross died on the cross' is a tautology. On the other hand, while faith is regarded as a species of belief, what makes this belief certain is its object, that what is believed is truth from God. Faith is not 'divine faith' because what is believed is regarded as being more likely to be true than not, but because it is regarded as something that God has said. It is God's saying that p that makes p certain.

[23] ibid., p. 58.

This requires qualification, for the last sentence as it stands is false. Supposing God says 'Jones says that Smith is dead', it does not follow that it is certain that Smith is dead. It is not God's saying a sentence that makes the sentence true, for it might be the reported speech of someone else. Rather it is God's *assertion* of p that makes p certain, his *promise* that p that makes p utterly reliable, and so forth. Thus the rule is 'If God asserts p, then p' is necessarily true whereas 'If Jones asserts p, then p' is not true; because Jones is fallible, but God is infallible. Jones may deceive, but God cannot.

This can be spelled out in terms of God's character or attributes. If complete truthfulness is an essential attribute of God,[24] then it is logically impossible for God to assert what is false, or what could turn out to be false. In Nelson Pike's terms, if p, then God believes p, and if God believes p, then p. If p is a proposition reporting some event, then that proposiiton is logically contingent. The event might not have happened, and the proposition could have been false. 'p, but possibly not p' is a true statement, where p is logically contingent. But suppose that it is known that God has asserted that p, where p is a report of some past event, then p is certainly true. To get clearer on the notion of certainty or necessity it is worth comparing the proposition 'God cannot lie' with 'God cannot fail to exist', that is, propositions claiming the necessary truthfulness of God with propositions concerning the necessary existence of God.

Anthony Kenny has suggested, in the context of the ontological argument, that the sense of necessity here is not logical necessity, but something like 'omni-temporal' necessity, which might be understood as 'If God exists at any time then he exists at any other time'; that is to say, the proposition 'God exists' has an unchangeable truth-value. When we consider propositions like 'God cannot lie' or 'God cannot err' what is being suggested is that these are to be understood in a similar way. (No doubt they are, as well, part of the 'grammar' of theism.) In 'God cannot err' God may be understood as having the ability to record infallibly, so that God's asserting that p entails the truth of p.

[24] For the notion of essential attribution applied to God, see Nelson Pike, *God and Timelessness* (1970).

H

That p has been revealed (asserted) by God who cannot lie does not affect the logical character of p, of course. If p refers to a contingent statement then not-p could still have been the case or could still be the case, logically speaking. Reformed theologians were perfectly familiar with this distinction.[25] No contradiction is involved in supposing that not-p, but given that the infallible recorder has recorded and revealed that p then p is epistemically certain, even though p may not be known comprehensively by human beings (on the grounds that p is a divine mystery). If p is epistemically certain then $-(-p$ is epistemically possible).

All this raises enormous problems about knowing what God has said, and hermeneutical problems about knowing what God means by what he says, though it is fair to say that those who take this view have not dodged these issues. For example, Owen has a book on hermeneutics entitled *Causes, Ways and Means of Understanding the Mind of God*.[26]

IV

The following states the central necessary condition of the model of religious belief sketched above :

A religiously believes p if A assents firmly to p (where p is taken to be revealed proposition) because A intuits, in grasping the meaning of p, that it is revealed by God. (As a matter of fact it is unrealistic to consider isolated propositions, for what is believed is a message composed of a variety of propositions. But this is neglected here.) Owen's position is not obsolete among contemporary Protestants. J. I. Packer makes the two familiar Owenian points, that faith is grounded in propositions that are not just probably true, and that what is peculiar to religious belief is that it is belief in the authority of God himself.

---

[25] 'It was decreed that wicked men should break the legs of the two thieves crucified with Christ, and that they should not break Christ's legs, yet the breaking of Christ's legs was in itself and from eternity no less possible, than the breaking of the legs of the fellow-sufferers with him; but God's only decree gave a futurition and an actual being to the one, not to the other'. Samuel Rutherford, *Christ Dying and Drawing Sinners to Himself* (1647), p 327.

[26] *Works*, ed. Goold, vol. 4.

'Faith, therefore, must rest on something more sure than as inference of probability . . . Articles of faith are just truths for which God is perceived to have vouched. It is fundamental to the nature of faith to take God's word for things; acceptance on the authority of God is the biblical analysis of faith on its intellectual side. The first manifestation of faith is cognitive : it appears in the recognition of affirmations made by men – prophets, apostles, the man Christ Jesus, any biblical writer – as truths uttered by God. Faith apprehends their testimony to God as being God's own testimony to Himself, and receives and responds to it as such.'[27]

This view of religious beliefs as certain, together with an epistemology that rests on intuition or 'illumination', enables a contrast to be made between faith and sight that cannot be made in anything like the same terms by the view of religious belief as belief in certain probabilities. For Locke and Butler the contrast between faith and sight must be between believing and knowing, whereas for Calvin or Owen the contrast is between believing the testimony of God, and taking account of the appearances of things. For Butler to believe *is* to go on the appearances of things, on what is probable judged by certain analogies, whereas (though there is no *a priori* connection between something being revealed by God and it being *im*probable), the model of belief of Owen and Calvin allows for this possibility, the possibility of trusting in the promises of God despite the present apparent non-fulfilment of them. This is an interesting practical religious difference between the two types.

In what sense is the certainty that attaches to this model of religious belief 'practical certainty'? In discussing the difficult notion of self-authentication the point was made that the certainty of the belief was not grounded in probabilities, but that it is in taking a given set of propositions to be certain (in the sense of being the assertions of God) that the distinctive religious needs of the individual are aroused, identified and satisfied.

The belief is practical, then, in the sense that what is believed has to do with the arousal and satisfaction of needs. But this does

[27] *'Fundamentalism' and the Word of God* (1958), pp. 117–8.

not mean that the belief is practical *either* because it is certain for all practical purposes, *or* because it is purely practical i.e. non-cognitive. Similarly, the propositions believed are not theoretical if by this is meant that their chief function is to satisfy the desire that men have for understanding and explaining their world. But they are cognitive in that the propositions believed purport to be informative of God and his purposes. The inference, characteristic of Kantian epistemology, 'If not theoretical, then not cognitive', is denied.

On this model, religious belief is for the believer knowledge *if* by this is meant justified true belief, though the justification is not justification in 'comprehensive' terms, nor is it one that every reasonable man would accept. Belief is 'ideological' knowledge in the sense defined in Chapter 4. The believer can give an account of the grounds of his belief that p, and in this sense the grounds are communicable, but they are not such as will inevitably bring any other reasonable man to believe in p. In this sense the knowledge claimed could be said to be 'non-natural'.

Such belief is very different from a belief that p based on the probability that p will happen or has happened, such beliefs being grounded perhaps in the analogies of nature or generalizations about human psychology. This would be belief, but not characteristically *religious* belief. It is not certain, but only probable, because it is grounded in conjectures about the past or future. Thomas Halyburton, an Owenian who defended the model of belief outlined in this chapter against Locke, put the point as follows :

'There is no reason for ranking all the truths therein delivered (viz. in the Bible) amongst those conjectural things that lean only on probabilities and reasonings from them which Mr Locke evidently does, while he sinks traditional revelation as to the point of certainty below our intuitive, rational and sensible knowledge; and banishes all faith, properly so called, out of the world, leaving no room for it, and substituting in its place an act of reason, proceeding upon probabilities, that is, on historical proofs, which he reckons only among probabilities.'[28]

[28] *The Works of Thomas Halyburton*, ed. Robert Burns (1835), p. 526.

The faith 'properly so called' that Halyburton claimed that Locke had banished, was belief in divine testimony.

Given this model of belief D. Z. Phillips might be just misinformed when he proceeds to draw certain general philosophical conclusions about the grammar of religious belief from the fact that the religious believer typically regards his beliefs as *certain*. It is not, as he suggests, simply a question of philosophers of religion forcing religious beliefs into an artificial dichotomy – *either* they express matters of fact *or* they express attitudes – which we need to be freed from by the Wittgensteinian 'look and see'.[29] Rather, the range of models of belief is much more varied than Phillips recognizes, and on one model, (the one discussed in this chapter), it makes sense to say that p is logically contingent (hypothetical), but that it can be known for certain, or believed with complete certainty.

It may be that when religious believers indicate the non-hypothetical character of their beliefs it is not because their beliefs are attitudes, but because they are beliefs in what is taken to be revealed, and so is utterly trustworthy. While the intuition they have that God has revealed such and such has consequences for the role that their religious beliefs play in their lives, the two are not to be thought of as logically equivalent. 'God has revealed p but Jones does not accept the meaningfulness of p' is not a self-contradiction for such people though perhaps 'God has revealed this but it has no significance for me' is, since *accepting* something as revealed has consequences. Perhaps it is the assimilation of such first- and third-person expressions that accounts for the attraction of certain kinds of reductionism in religion.

[29] J. R. Jones and D. Z. Phillips, 'Belief and Loss of Belief – A Discussion', *Sophia* (March 1970). Reprinted in *Faith and Philosophical Enquiry*, ed. D. Z. Phillips (1970).

7

REGULATION

The models of religious belief discussed in the previous two chapters have significant differences, particularly on the question of the grounds for belief. But they have in common the view that what makes a belief *religious* is its distinctive content. 'Belief', that is, figures in both models as a cognitive expression. The view now to be considered, Immanuel Kant's, holds that what makes a belief religious is its *regulative* character, the fact that it has a certain sort of influence over a person's conduct, particularly his moral conduct. However, this does not mean that *any* belief could be regulative. Only belief in a purely-moral God, whose existence is necessitated by the requirements of morality, will serve. Religious belief has nothing to do, in a positive sense, with knowledge. Kant denies knowledge, in order to make room for faith.

Kant has become the head of a tradition; though the positive part of his thesis has been continually amended and refined by Protestant continental theologians from Schleiermacher to Bultmann, they all accept the negative claim of the critical philosophy that it is impossible to have knowledge of God. And though in this chapter the focus of our attention will be on Kant, it is on him as representative of a type. Two inter-connected questions will occupy us:

(*a*) What does Kant mean by calling belief in God 'regulative'?

(*b*) In what sense can Kant be said to hold that God exists? After attempting to answer these questions it will be argued that Kant's views have certain affinities to those of the 'later' Wittgenstein, so far as we possess them.

I

Kant's view of religious belief as regulative must be set against his rejection of speculative theology as a fruitless way of providing men with a knowledge of God. To use the principles of reason to discover facts about a supreme being would be to employ them transcendentally, when they allow only of an immanent use. Or, to put another argument used, if it is possible to use some feature of experience, say, that events cause other events, to construct a proof of the existence of God, then the God whose existence was established by means of such a proof would be an object of experience, and like all such objects of experience would necessarily be conditioned under the forms of space and time. And this would be an absurd supposition in the case of God. 'Transcendental questions allow only of transcendental answers', that is, they allow answers that use only *a priori* concepts. But it is impossible to get to know about God (that is, come to know the truth of certain synthetic propositions) by means of the use of concepts that are exclusively *a priori*, for synthetic *a priori* knowledge only 'expresses the formal conditions of a possible experience'.[1]

Here it is not in the least important whether these claims are valid ones, but only that Kant accepted them, and that they allowed him, or drove him, to argue that the propositions of speculative metaphysics have a non-cognitive function and justification. While the existence of God cannot be established by the arguments of transcendental metaphysics, God is a necessary postulate of the practical reason.

Besides these general epistemological arguments, Kant has a specific argument against the idea of religious belief as assent, as follows : if proposition p is reported by A to B then necessarily, (if the report is not chimerical, or otherwise spurious), A experienced what p refers to, or if *he* did not experience it himself, he received p on testimony from someone who did. However long the chain of testimony, eventually it stops when someone experiences for himself what the proposition p refers to. Thus p is experienced, and is therefore empirical – a fact of geography, say. While, it is, practically speaking, impossible to know certain geographical or historical facts for ourselves, it is logically possible to know them. 'Objects of history and geography, like everything in general which it is at least possible to know by the constitution of our cognitive faculties, belong not to things of faith but to

---

[1] *Critique of Pure Reason*, trans. Norman Kemp Smith, p. 529.

things of fact.'[2] It is this argument that underlies Kant's distinction between historical/ecclesiastical faith and pure religious faith in *Religion Within the Limits of Reason Alone*. So religious faith is not a species of belief on testimony, for testimony is distinguishable from knowledge only by contingent factors. It could be knowledge. But faith could not be knowledge. Hence faith cannot be, or include, belief as assent to testimony.

The objects of religious faith must therefore be objects of pure reason, that is to say, pure practical reason. With respect to such objects it is not possible to have either cognitive certainty or cognitive uncertainty. Such belief is a purely practical affair, necessarily so. It 'proves nothing for theoretical pure rational cognition',[3] and, it can be added, it requires no cognitive foundation.

'The cognition of the latter (viz. the highest Object of all moral laws) is neither knowledge nor opinion of the being and character of these conditions, (viz. the conditions under which we think this possibility is postulated) regarded as theoretical cognition; but is a mere assumption in a reference which is practical and commanded for the moral use of our Reason.'[4]

Belief in God, as a postulate of the pure practical reason, is 'inevitable'. It is a belief which nothing can shake, for if *per impossible* it were shaken, then the individual's moral principles would be completely overthrown, and he would cease to be a moral agent. For it is necessary to postulate the existence of God in order to secure the systematic unity of the ends of morality. By this Kant appears to mean not that a virtuous atheist is a contradiction in terms, but that the virtuous atheist cannot have as a goal the achieving of the *summum bonum*, where happiness is proportioned to virtue, and which it is the duty of men to promote. Only God can bring about the *summum bonum*, and yet the moral agent has an interest in having this brought about, and will do all in his power to see that it is achieved. But if the moral agent is an atheist, and does not believe that God will bring about the *summum bonum* because he does not believe in God, then his own effort to achieve it will be put in jeopardy.

[2] *Critique of Judgement*, trans. Bernard, p. 407.
[3] op. cit., p. 407.
[4] op. cit., p. 408.

W. H. Walsh puts it in this way: 'If we come to believe that whatever we do and however hard we try the chances are that our ultimate end will never be attained, our moral effort will clearly be seriously weakened. Should we conclude that there is *no* possibility of its accomplishment, we must abandon the whole endeavour as futile.'[5] Whether the connection of moral effort with belief in the *summum bonum* is a contingent psychological one, as Walsh seems to think it is, or logically necessary, is worth pausing to consider for the light it may throw on Kant's view of the certainty of religious belief.

On the one hand Kant wishes to hold that without the idea that virtue will be rewarded the moral agent will relax his effort. God's existence cannot be doubted and people still pursue their duty with unremitting vigilance. This seems to make the idea of the *summum bonum*, and of God as the provider of it, a psychological necessity. Coming to believe in God, on this view, would be coming to believe that moral effort is not in vain but will be rewarded. But if this is Kant's view, it is hard to see how it makes God's existence certain or 'inevitable'.

On the other hand Kant may be offering a thesis about the meaning of 'moral'. 'Jones constantly endeavours to do his duty' *means* 'Jones believes in God.' Yet if Kant means this, it is hard to see how he can raise the possibility of the virtuous atheist for discussion, as he does when discussing 'Spinoza' in the *Critique of Judgement*,[6] or allow that a man can be virtuous while not pursuing the *summum bonum*. It appears that, in regarding the existence of God as a 'postulate' of the pure practical reason, Kant was searching for some connection between morality and belief in God that was neither contingent nor necessary. But what could such a connection be?

Practical reason secures the existence of God where theoretical proofs, in attempting to pass beyond the limits of all experience, end in failure. 'No one, indeed, will be able to boast that he *knows* that there is a God, and a future life; if he knows this, he is the very man for whom I have long (and vainly) sought.'[7]

---

[5] 'Kant's Moral Theology', *Proceedings of the British Academy*, vol. 49 (1963), p. 272.
[6] *Critique of Judgement*, pp. 120–1.
[7] *Critique of Pure Reason*, p. 650.

Asserted as a cognitive proposition 'God exists' is epistemologically impossible but as an unknowable postulate of pure practical reason it is necessary and certain.

II

In what sense can Kant be said to assert the existence of God? Trancendental ideas are fruitless if considered referentially, but they have a perfectly proper *immanent* use, not as referential and cognitive but as moral and regulative. Another way of putting this is that for Kant moral belief requires belief in the reality of the objects of the transcendental ideas. Nevertheless it is not possible either to prove or disprove that there are objects corresponding to these ideas. To attempt such a proof would be to allow the possibility of theoretical knowledge of that which is unknowable. The fine distinction that Kant draws, and needs to draw, between notions that are not cognitive and referential and that yet are not merely figments, is of considerable importance in trying to make a proper estimate of the existential import of his notion of religious belief, the sense in which he can be said to be a reductionist in theology.

In the Appendix to the 'Ideal of Pure Reason' Kant has some interesting remarks on the sense in which God may be said to exist. He argues, first, that God must be said to be distinct from the world, 'For the world is a sum of appearances; and there must therefore be some transcendental ground of the appearances, that is, a ground which is thinkable only by the pure understanding.'[8] Secondly, he goes on to ask whether this transcendental ground is a substance, and answers that this is a meaningless question, because the concepts in terms of which an attempt is made to characterize such a transcendental substance would have to be entirely empirical (the only cognitive concepts we possess), and these 'have no meaning whatsoever when not applied to objects of possible experience, that is, to the world of sense'.[9]

In trying to get a little clearer on this question, some progress might be made by comparing the things that Kant says about 'God' with what he says about 'noumenon'. For Kant 'God' has the same status as 'noumenon' in that both words denote some

[8] op. cit., p. 565.   [9] ibid., p. 566.

non-phenomenal reality. This means that ordinary empirical predicates cannot be applied to God; there are no concepts available to speak of God. All that can be said of him (cognitively) is that he exists, and whatever analytically follows from this, e.g. 'God is simple', 'God is infinite'.

By comparison, when Kant tries to justify talk of noumena, things in themselves, for the existence of which there is no moral requirement as there is with God, then he is on weak ground, as Jonathan Bennett points out.[10] Kant's argument is that, if the existence of noumena is denied, we are committed to saying that there can be appearances (phenomena), which are not appearances *of* anything. Bennett shows that what 'empirical things are appearances' means is that statements about material things can be wholly analysed in experiential terms, and that this does not require something of which the appearances are appearances. Further, Kant is not using 'God' purely negatively, as Bennett says he uses 'noumenon', at least on some occasions.[11] Kant, that is, is not using 'God' simply to draw attention to the limits of our sensibility, but to make positive existential claims.

The answer to the question, Does belief in God carry existential import? is a qualified yes. But the belief involved is of a rather odd kind, for the object of belief could never become an object of knowledge, unlike a belief in the Abominable Snowman. So that 'belief' is not a straightforward cognitive term. Yet Kant's treatment of the existence of God is not straightforwardly reductionist either, at least in those contexts in which he regards belief in the existence of God as necessary for morality. It is not that Kant regards belief in God's existence as logically equivalent to a set of human moral dispositions. Kant's view that belief in God is necessary for morals is worked out most fully in the Second *Critique*, but in the First *Critique* he speaks of the postulation of the existence of God 'in order that through such agency effect may be given' to the laws of morals. That is, not merely that God is to be postulated as the rewarder of virtue (this is mentioned prominently—relatively—in the First *Critique*, and less prominently in the Second, finally being dropped in *Religion Within the Limits of Reason Alone*), but that since

[10] *Kant's Analytic* (1966), p. 25.
[11] ibid., pp. 57–8.

morality commands the *summum bonum* it must be possible, and yet it would be impossible if God did not exist.

Kant wishes to say both that God exists, and that nothing can be known about him. But he is left in an odd position, for while he refuses to allow the question 'Is God a substance?' to be asked, he answers the question 'Is God the transcendental ground of all appearances?' with a bold affirmative.

While Kant allows that God's existence can never be known, he does claim that it is true that God exists. In the interesting section *How is it possible to conceive of extending pure reason in a practical respect without thereby extending its knowledge as speculative?*,[12] Kant acknowledges that the practical law postulates the existence of God, the objective reality of which cannot be shown by speculative reason. He distinguishes, that is, between the theoretical and the speculative reason. The theoretical reason, as was shown above, postulates God's existence, and so 'gains an accession'. But though through this accession theoretical reason is extended, the speculative reason is not. 'A positive use cannot be made of those objects for theoretical purposes', for all that is known is the theoretical necessity of God for pure practical reason. No intuitions of God, that is to say no theoretical knowledge of God, is thereby given. The postulates of pure practical reason – God, freedom and immortality – are not cognitions, they are 'transcendent thoughts', that cannot be expressed in terms of synthetic *a posteriori* propositions.

'It was therefore no extension of knowledge of given supersensuous objects, but still an extension of theoretical reason and of its knowledge with respect to the supersenuous in general, inasmuch as knowledge is compelled to concede that there are such objects without more exactly defining them, and thus without being able to extend this knowledge of objects given to it only on practical grounds for only practical use.'[13]

Though it cannot be pretended that this makes the previous puzzles over Kant's views any clearer, it does make clear that 'I believe in God' has existential import for Kant, and gives further

---

[12] *Critique of Practical Reason*, ed. L. W. Beck (1963), p. 227.
[13] ibid., p. 237.

grounds for rejecting Walsh's view that Braithwaite and Kant have 'fundamentally the same view'.

Kant's view of *religion* is, in the terminology introduced in Chapter 2, 'weak reductionism'. He regards the traditional claims of Christianity, for example, as religiously irrelevant. His view of *God*, on the other hand, is non-reductionist. He does not regard 'God' as equivalent to a set of moral *dispositions*. That such a God exists can be known theoretically though nothing about God can be known speculatively. In this sole respect does his use of 'belief' follow normal cognitive usage in carrying existential import. But, having allowed 'space' for affirming the existence of God, Kant can allow himself no more space in which God might be known.

Further, not only can God not be known, but also for Kant certain traditionally Christian predicates of God are religiously unimportant : those that comprise 'ecclesiastical' as opposed to 'pure religious' faith. Hence Kant's moral theology leads immediately to religion, defined by him both in the third *Critique* and in *Religion Within the Limits of Reason Alone* as 'the recognition of all duties as divine commands'. Religion follows immediately from the recognition that the duties of morality are the commands of God. Though Kant does not reduce theology to ethics, he does reduce religion to morality.

To say that Kant himself has no interest in a non-moral theology is not to say that his critical philosophy *as such* commits one to this view of theology. Kant's arguments against a speculative-metaphysical knowledge of God do not of themselves entail a rejection of revelation, though Kant himself did reject revelation. In fact G. C. Storr (1746–1805) argued that a revelation was a requirement of the practical reason, and attempted to argue on *a posteriori* grounds that the New Testament was credible as a revelation from God.[14]

Modifying Locke's famous remark about substance it might be said that for Kant God is 'Something, I know not *that*'. Put theologically, Kant's doctrine of God is necessarily deistic. God is, precisely, a ground; no changes in the world can be known either as the acts of God or the words of God, for if, for the

---

[14] G. C. Storr, *Annotationes quaedom Theologicae ad Philosophicam Kantii de Religione Doctrinam* (1793).

general epistemological reasons we have glanced at, 'God is good' is to be regarded as regulative and not as a constitutive principle – as, crudely, moral and not factual – then *a fortiori* propositions such as 'God spoke to Moses' and 'God made the bush burn' cannot be known to be propositions about the words and acts of God.

It is true that in the *Lectures on Philosophical Theology* Kant denies that he is a deist. The deist, he says, 'understands by the concept of God merely a blindly working eternal nature, as the root of all things, a primorial being or a highest cause of the world'. By contrast, he calls his own position 'moral theism'. 'Theism consists in believing not merely in a God, but also in a living God, who has produced the world through knowledge and free volition.'[15] Allen Wood adds that according to Kant it is possible to *trust* God, and so his conception of God cannot be deistic.[16] It can be granted that Kant wishes to ascribe purposes to God, for instance the rewarding of the virtuous and the punishing of the vicious, and to allow for religious relations between God and men. But then so did some at least of the English deists, with their emphasis on 'natural religion'. The point of calling Kant a deist, despite his own dislike of the word, is that both for him and the English deists God cannot be active in the world in any sense in which his actions can be identified as such.

In this connection it seems to be mistaken to compare classical theism and the theology of J. A. T. Robinson with Locke and Berkeley on substance, as Stuart C. Brown has done,[17] and indeed as Robinson himself has done. Robinson states that he came

'to the same sort of point which Bishop Berkeley reached in his questioning of Locke's philosophy of substance. Was it really essential, in order to assert the fact of being held in this inescapable personal relationship as the final interpretative reality of life, to posit this concept of a divine Person behind the scenes?[18]

But what the shift from Locke to Berkeley represents is not that from theism to some reductionist view, but from deism, the deism of Kant, belief in a divine Person who is *necessarily* 'behind the scenes' to some kind of reductionism in which talk of such a

[15] This and the previous quotation are taken from Allen Wood, *Kant's Moral Religion* (1970), p. 164.   [16] ibid., p. 161.
[17] *Do Religious Claims Make Sense?* (1969), pp. 156–7.
[18] Quoted by Brown, op. cit., p. 157.

divine Person (Locke's substance) is translated into talk of personal relationships (Berkeley's *percipi*). If Robinson regards his transition analogously to the shift between Locke and Berkeley, what he has abandoned is deism, not classical Christian theism in which God not only upholds the phenomena but also himself actively intervenes in redemption and judgment. Robinson's transition is, as Alasdair MacIntyre has pointed out, a case of the twentieth-century rejecting post-Enlightenment views of God.[19]

III

In the lecture already referred to, W. H. Walsh has drawn attention to certain respects in which the views of Kant and Wittgenstein on religion coincide. It will now be argued that while there are obvious enough differences between the two, the similarities are striking. Besides the intrinsic interest of this comparison it will be significant for the thesis of the book because of the use to which Wittgenstein's views on religion have been put by some philosophers of religion more recently, as a response to the charge that religious language is meaningless.

While Kant attempted to plot the boundaries of knowledge Wittgenstein was concerned with the boundaries of meaning, with the limits of what could be said. This is true both of the 'earlier' and 'later' Wittgenstein. For example, in the *Tractatus* he held that 'the mystical' could not be spoken about. In the *Investigations* he rejects the idea that there could be a language of sensations independent of the language of material objects. For Kant, on the other hand, certain unanswerable questions force themselves on men, requiring to be asked.

While, as we have seen, for Kant God has the ontological status of a noumenon, in the later Wittgenstein there is a complete departure from the empiricist and phenomenalist analysis in terms of substance and attributes, or noumenon and phenomena, and instead an analysis in terms of language-games. 'God' is not given a meaning in contrast to phenomena, but it is given a meaning within the language-game of religion in contrast to some other language-game, that of science, say.

[19] 'The Fate of Theism', in Paul Ricoer and Alasdair MacIntyre, *The Religious Significance of Atheism* (1969).

Further, for Wittgenstein in his later period religion is no longer transcendent *in the sense that* it transcends the limits of language as in the *Tractatus*. But this is not to say that in his later period he conceives of religion in immanentistic terms. Certainly the 'objectivity' of religion (as David Pears puts it)[20] is lost, and religion becomes one part of his 'linguistic naturalism'. Objectivism collapses into anthropocentrism. But it is, or at any rate may be, a feature of the language-game of religion that it has a non-hypothetical, non-contingent (and in *this* sense transcendent) character.

A final significant point of contrast is that, while Kant has developed an original, complex theory of religion, Wittgenstein appears reluctant to put over his own view at any length, which means that piecing together his view may be somewhat hazardous. The materials we possess are fragmentary, and mostly second-hand. Some may object that Wittgenstein's religious views are irrelevant. In which case what follows should be understood as a discussion of Wittgenstein's attempt to preserve certain 'forms of life' from encroachment.

Some may wish to say that these differences, large enough in all conscience, make comparison between the two futile. This is an understandable point of view. However, the attempt will now be made to argue in the other direction, and to show that for Wittgenstein, as for Kant, religious belief is a regulative notion. It will be argued that in his later period,[21] Wittgenstein held the following three theses:

(*a*) That religious beliefs are not hypotheses or inductive generalizations.

(*b*) That religious beliefs are regulative.

[20] *Wittgenstein* (1971), p. 169.

[21] This applies to his remarks on religious belief in *Lectures and Conversations on Aesthetics, Psychology and Religious Belief*, ed. Cyril Barrett (1966) and his remarks on Frazer's *Golden Bough* (*Synthese* 17, No. 3, 1967: English translation by A. C. Miles and Rush Rhees, *The Human World* (No. 3, May 1971). All references are to this translation). The parallel between Wittgenstein's earlier views on religion in the *Tractatus* and Kant's moral theology will not be examined here. If anything, in view of Wittgenstein's belief in the 'objectivity' of religion in this period the parallelism between Wittgenstein and Kant is even more striking. Erik Stenius, *Wittgenstein's Tractatus* (1961), ch. 11 and David Pears, *Wittgenstein* (1971), pp. 35, 45ff, have both drawn attention to the parallel between Kant and the *Tractatus*.

(c) That religious beliefs are non-isolable.

Though distinguishable, these theses are not in fact separable elements in Wittgenstein's view.

The main differences between them, besides the important ones already noted, are that Wittgenstein held a different view from Kant on the connection betwen religious belief and morality, and on the question of the loss of religious belief. These differences are important, but not so important as to take Wittgenstein out of an essentially Kantian position.

We shall begin by discussing the third thesis, the (as yet not very clear) claim that religious belief is non-isolable.

According to Wittgenstein the difference between believer and non-believer is not simply that one believes p while the other believes −p. In religious discussion, as opposed to discussion about matters of fact, there is an absence of contradiction.

'Suppose someone were a believer and said : "I believe in a Last Judgement", and I said : "Well, I'm not sure. Possibly." You would say that there is an enormous gulf between us. If he said "There is a German aeroplane overhead", and I said "Possibly, I'm not so sure" you'd say we were fairly near.'[22]

This point about the non-self-contradictoriness of opposite religious beliefs is that it is like the kind of disagreement between someone who maintains that chairs are real, and someone who asserts that they are not. Their disagreement is not about particular features of chairs – whether all chairs have backs, for example – or about the meaning of the English word 'chair', but about the status of a whole range of expressions about chairs. Someone who denies that chairs are real is not affirming that they are unreal, but that it makes no sense to say either that they are real or unreal. The disagreement is peculiar because it is not within a language-game, but across one.

Wittgenstein would have said, at one time, that to affirm the reality of chairs is to come up against the 'limits of language'. Such 'external' affirmations are part of the mythology of language. They are not on that account pointless, but their point must be found elsewhere than in, for example, science or history.

[22] *Lectures and Conservations on Aesthetics, Psychology and Religious Belief*, ed. Cyril Barrett (1966), p. 53.

I

Disagreement of the sort just discussed occurs when one of the participants in the conversation has misunderstood the distinctive role or point of religious language. To understand religion is to understand a language. To misunderstand is not like misunderstanding a *word* in a language, it is to fail to understand the whole language. Truly to explain (i.e. show the significance of) religion or magic, one has to show its connexion with certain values or happenings (e.g. birth, death, love, hatred), and not to offer hypotheses about its origins, or to regard religion or magic as offering quasi-scientific hypotheses about e.g. how to make rain, or to survive death.

So that Wittgenstein's remarks about the Last Judgement only make sense if sentences about the Last Judgement are regarded as being in a different language-game from sentences about the markings of aeroplanes. The Last Judgement is regarded as a component part in some pattern of belief which is in a different language-game from language about material objects. According to Wittgenstein 'belief' is being used differently from its use in material-object contexts involving generalizations, for example.[23]

The upshot of Wittgenstein's remarks is that the two – the affirmation of the Last Judgement, and its denial – are 'on an entirely different plane'.[24] Presumably the point of contrasting belief in the Resurrection with the belief that the aeroplane is German is that the latter is an independently identifiable particular. That is to say, it can be identified as an aeroplane, and the question can be raised 'Is it a German aeroplane?' 'That is an aeroplane but is it a German one?' makes sense. That there is a (possibly German) aeroplane above already presupposes a common language-game with which certain particulars have already been identified. Hence disagreement in the detailed description of the particular – one person thinking it is a German aeroplane, the other having doubts – means that the two are 'fairly near' in that there are sets of descriptions that they would both be agreed on. The examples that Wittgenstein uses suit,

[23] Whether Wittgenstein is correct in his account of what religious believers would do or say is omitted from consideration at this point. It may be that his views as to what people would say in these contexts are already heavily impregnated with what he takes the correct account of religious language to be.

[24] *Lectures and Conversations*, p. 53.

to some extent, the point he is trying to make because referring to the aeroplane is a case of referring to something contemporaneous with the speakers, while referring to the Last Judgement is not. Another way that Wittgenstein has of putting this is to say that religious beliefs are not comparable because they do not have comparable grounds.

On this interpretation of Wittgenstein's remarks he would be committed to saying that there could be cases in which different religious beliefs were 'fairly near'. Wittgenstein, on this view, is not saying that it is a necessary feature of the language-game or language-games of religion that there is an 'enormous gulf' between any two religious views.

Other remarks made by Wittgenstein suggest a different view.

'You might be surprised that there hasn't been opposed to those who believe in Resurrection those who say "Well, possibly".'

'Here believing obviously plays much more this role : suppose we said that a certain picture might play the role of constantly admonishing me, or I always think of it. Here, an enormous difference would be between those people for whom the picture is constantly in the foreground, and the others who just didn't use it at all.

'Those who said : "Well, possibly it may happen and possibly not" would be on an entirely different plane.'[25]

These suggest the view that what makes a belief religious is not whether it figures in the same language-game as material objects but *the difference it makes*, and that the 'Possibly, I'm not sure', said of the idea that the aeroplane above is German indicates indifference, the absence of that commitment which is characteristic of religious beliefs.

It may seem that these two possibilities are exclusive of each other; that Wittgenstein thinks that what makes a belief religious is *either* its being in a distinctive language-game, *or* the sort of difference that the belief makes to the life of the believer. However, it would appear that he thinks that these are two ways of saying the same thing; that part of what it means for a belief to be religious is that it has a certain effect, or role, in a person's life.

But there is no entailment here; there are cases where a belief

[25] ibid., p. 56.

gets its religious force because the believer takes what he believes to be not simply a picture that admonishes, but an event in the material-object world, either present or future. Such beliefs are logically contingent, and observable in principle, though they are not empirical beliefs in the sense that they have been discovered by a process of inductive generalization, or that they are hypotheses based entirely on such generalizations.

The snatch of conversation that Wittgenstein gives about the Resurrection could well take place between someone who holds that the Last Judgement is both an event to be looked forward to in the material world ('every eye shall see him') and an event the significance of which could only be appreciated by taking into account other beliefs, themselves interpretative of events in the material world. In these circumstances someone who doubts the Last Judgement might fairly be said to be doubting the truth of the web of doctrines of which it is a part, and to be 'on an entirely different plane' from the believer. Alternatively, the conversation might be taken to be one between believers about a doctrine. Then one would have to deny Wittgenstein's verdict that the two were poles apart. (*The First Letter to the Corinthians*, Chapter 15, gives instances of these last two possibilities, or suggests a framework in which they are plausible.)

Whatever the other possibilities, Wittgenstein's position is that religious belief has entirely 'different connections' from empirical belief, so that to regard the Last Judgement as a prediction amounts to a failure to grasp the grammar of religion, and is not just a 'blunder' or 'mistake' within religion.[26]

The idea that religious belief is non-isolable, that it forms part of a distinctive 'form of life' is closely connected in Wittgenstein's mind with thesis (1) above, the non-inductive, categorical character of religious belief, on which it is necessary to make some further remarks. But this view cannot really be separated from (2), the idea of religious belief as regulative. So Wittgenstein says, about the claim that Christianity rests on a historical basis, 'It has been said a thousand times by intelligent people

[26] ibid., p. 58–9. Compare with Wittgenstein's remarks on mistakes and blunders in *On Certainty*, paras. 304, 425, 650–1, 659, 660–676 etc., and his comment on Frazer, 'Frazer's account of the magical and religious notions of men is unsatisfactory: it makes these notions appear as *mistakes*'. 'Remarks', p. 28.

that indubitability is not enough in this case. Even if there is as much evidence as for Napoleon. Because the indubitability wouldn't be enough to make me change my whole life.'[27] This seems to be the argument that because empirical beliefs and dubitable and religious beliefs indubitable religious beliefs cannot be, or contain, empirical beliefs. Even where they seem to, as when religious people refer to the life of Christ, the events are not treated by the believers *as* historical, empirical events. Religious beliefs are unshakeable, or what may be termed categorical. 'Asking him is not enough. He will probably say he has proof. But he has what you might call an unshakeable belief.'[28] That is, what makes a belief religious is the sort of 'hold' that it has over the believer.

In 'Remarks on Frazer's *Golden Bough*' the point about the non-inductive character of religious and magical beliefs is put in the form of a thesis about explanation. Frazer has misunderstood primitive magic because he has taken it to be primitive physics and has 'explained' it genetically. 'An historical explanation, an explanation as an hypothesis of the development, is only *one* kind of summary of the data – of their synopsis. We can equally well see the data in their relations to one another and make a summary of them in a general picture without putting it in the form of a hypothesis regarding the temporal development.'[29]

The parallel between Kant and Wittgenstein so far should be apparent. Both wish to make a sharp distinction between material-object beliefs and religious beliefs, though on different grounds; to stress the peculiar certainty or unshakeableness that attaches to religious belief; and to avoid a 'hard reductionist' position in which religious propositions become *nothing but* expressions of moral intent. Wittgenstein avoids this by stressing the autonomy of religious belief and the internality of the truth-conditions of religion, and Kant by emphasizing the (rather peculiar and elusive) 'objectivity' of God. And both wish to say that what is characteristic of religious belief is its regulative character. Wittgenstein speaks explicitly of the 'regulating' character of religious belief.[30]

[27] *Lectures and Conversations*, p. 57.   [28] ibid., pp. 53–4.
[29] 'Remarks', p. 34.   [30] *Lectures and Conversations*, p. 54.

Thesis (*b*) can be brought out most effectively by considering two passages in the *Lectures and Conversations*. The first of these is where he imagines someone making belief in the Last Judgement guidance for his life. That is, 'Whenever he does anything, this is before his mind.'[31] Wittgenstein describes this regulative role as follows :

'Suppose you had two people, and one of them, when he had to decide which course to take, thought of retribution, and the other did not. One person might, for instance, be inclined to take everything that happened to him as a reward or punishment, and another person doesn't think of this at all.'[32]

It is not that 'believing in the Last Judgement' is to be taken to mean 'taking everything that happens as a reward or punishment'; the two are not logically equivalent. Wittgenstein is clear on this, and in general on the non-reducibility or non-analysability of such language. Thus :

'Suppose someone, before going to China, when he might never see me again, said to me : 'We might see one another after death" – would I necessarily say that I don't understand him? I might say (want to say) simply, "Yes. I *understand* him entirely".

'*Lewy* "In this case, you might only mean that he expressed a certain attitude".

'I would say "No, it isn't the same as saying 'I'm very fond of you' " – and it may not be the same as saying anything else. It says what it says. Why should you be able to substitute anything else ?'[33]

If 'Jones believes in the Last Judgement' is not to be analysed as 'Jones has such and such attitudes' how is it to be understood? It would seem that to believe *religiously* in the Last Judgement is for the 'picture' of the Last Judgement to have a certain 'hold' over one's life. It is the *idea* of the Judgement 'before one's mind' that affects one's life, not the belief in the coming *event*. Yet if the Last Judgement is not regarded by the believer, according to Wittgenstein, as a coming event, it is hard to see how his

[31] ibid., p. 53.
[32] ibid., p. 54.
[33] ibid., pp. 70–1.

account can be non-reductionist, at least in the sense that believing in the Last Judgement comes to mean having certain attitudes, though perhaps not moral attitudes.

The second context is his remarks about immortality, which have a strongly Kantian flavour about them.

'A great writer said that, when he was a boy, his father set him a task, and he suddenly felt that nothing, not even death, could take away the responsibility (in doing this task); this was his duty to do, and that even death couldn't stop it being his duty. He said that this was, in a way, a proof of the immortality of the soul – because if this lives on (the responsibility won't die). The idea is given by what we call the proof.'[34]

It appears that Wittgenstein is not saying that 'having an immortal soul' is equivalent to 'believing that there are duties that death cannot remove'. Yet he does not appear to be saying that the belief in such duties necessitates (in some way) the immortality of the soul. The difficulty in making any sense of these remarks, if they are neither reductionist nor involving any empirical content, is very great – particularly so, because of Wittgenstein's insistence on the *sui generis* character of religion, and the consequent lack of pressure to make his meaning clear. Yet despite these difficulties Wittgenstein takes the transcendent-sounding language of religion to be understandable primarily in regulative terms, in immanentistic terms, and makes a close connection with moral notions such as duty and the sense of personal responsibility.

The regulative or non-theoretical character of religious belief is expressed by Wittgenstein in his remarks on Frazer's *Golden Bough* by saying that there can be no error in religion ('a religious symbol does not rest on any opinion. And error belongs only with opinion'), and by denying that rituals have a causally efficacious character. 'Burning an effigy. Kissing the picture of a loved one. This is obviously not based on a belief that it will have a definite effect on the object which the picture represents. It aims at some satisfaction and it achieves it. Or rather, it does not *aim* at anything; we act in this way and then feel satisfied.'[35]

It seems that the particular expression that religion takes,

[34] ibid., p. 70. [35] 'Remarks', p. 31.

belief in the Last Judgement in some cases, belief in something else in the case of primitive tribes, is a matter of convention or of historical accident. To what extent is hard to say, for there is some connection between the notion of the Last Judgement and the sense of personal responsibility, and there are some 'pictures' that could not have religious connections (presumably). Yet Wittgenstein seems to leave open the idea that other 'pictures' would do the particular regulative job as well. This is similar to the Kantian contrast between pure religious faith and ecclesiastical faith, and Kant's comment in *Religion Within the Limits of Reason Alone*, that there may be a historical connection between particular historical or ecclesiastical doctrines and pure religious faith, in that pure faith arises as a matter of fact through various historical religions, but that pure religious faith is to be understood as logically independent of any particular historical or ecclesiastical claims.

In a paper on Wittgenstein's notion of religious belief[36] W. D. Hudson points to the regulative function of religious belief according to Wittgenstein, as others have done,[37] and makes the point that, while the meaning of an expression may be simply regulative or heuristic, (the principle that every event has a cause, for example), the regulative character of other expressions may derive from their factual character, and the regulative character of many expressions undoubtedly does. That is to say, factual utterances have operational consequences. 'It is midwinter' has in some countries the operational consequence 'Expect a hard frost tonight', and belief that it is midwinter might be said to have 'regulative consequences' for a whole range of human behaviour. To make the point that religious discourse is regulative is not *ipso facto* to make the point that it does not involve any use of material-object language, but to draw attention to the fact that, as Berkeley would put it, some religious language 'terminates in the will'.

So far the similarities between Wittgenstein and Kant have been stressed. There are two important differences, besides those mentioned earlier, between their views of religion. Wittgenstein

---

[36] *Talk of God*, ed. G. N. A. Vesey, p. 36ff.
[37] e.g. Ninian Smart in *Philosophers and Religious Truth* (Second Edition, 1969).

does not think that his remarks on religion or his account of religious belief constitute a proof of God's existence in any sense. The idea of proving the existence of God is ruled out by his appeal to the autonomous character of religious language. Secondly, as was noted in the discussion of Kant's views, Kant stresses that pure religious faith has a certainty and irretractability about it because of its close connection with pure practical reason, although he is not very clear what this connection is.

Though Wittgenstein stresses that for the believer belief is unshakeable, he does not seem to rule out the phenomenon of loss of religious belief. At least, though he does not say this in so many words, the extrapolations of his view made by D. Z. Phillips[38] seem entirely reasonable. This is not the place to go into the difficult and much-discussed question of the relation between faith and understanding (for this, see the last chapter), but the fact that according to Phillips scepticism is to be understood as the decline in the 'hold' that a picture has over the lives of people, is worth recording. This loss will affect how the individual 'sees life' if it is true, as Wittgenstein claims, that believing in the Last Judgement involves seeing one's life in terms of retribution and reward. But as religion is not as vitally connected with morality as it is for Kant, loss of belief will not have the same bearing on morals as, on Kant's view, loss of belief has.

IV

The aim of this chapter has been to show that Kant and (to a lesser extent) Wittgenstein provide a model of religious belief that is distinct from religious belief understood as belief in certain probabilities, or belief in divine revelation or testimony, or from a 'hard' reductionism position such as that of Braithwaite. On the Kantian view *A religiously believes when he regards his duties as divine commands; religious belief is practical in that God can only be spoken of as being believed in in non-cognitive contexts.* 'God' refers to an unknowable moral-metaphysical substrate required by the practical reason. For Wittgenstein a belief is *religious* when it has certain characteristic connections; these

[38] In a discussion with J. R. Jones, 'Belief and Loss of Belief – A Discussion', *Sophia* (March 1970).

connections play a role in enabling the believer to regulate his life with respect to his own personal responsibility, or death. There are of course many differences between the two philosophers, but this regulative understanding of religious belief is something distinctive held in common.

At the outset of this chapter it was suggested that Kant is at the head of a whole post-Kantian tradition in Protestant theology, influential particularly on the continent of Europe, from Schleiermacher to Bultmann. Though they differ markedly amongst themselves, they address themselves to a programme that only makes sense on the presuppositions of Kantian epistemology, the programme of analysing religious belief (or Christian faith) in immanentist terms – in terms of ethical values (Ritschl) or existential decision (Bultmann) or secularity (Bonhoeffer). Religious belief is in each of these cases non-cognitive, and so invulnerable to attack. Its certainty is, in Paul Tillich's words 'independent of the unavoidable uncertainties of historical faith'[39] This view of religious belief as something independent of history influences the attitude of such people to the criticism of the documents of Christianity, and so Bultmann can say :

'I have never yet felt uncomfortable with my radical criticism; on the contrary, I have been entirely comfortable. But I often have the impression that my conservative New Testament colleagues feel very uncomfortable, for I see them perpetually engaged in salvage operations. I calmly let the fire burn, for I see that what is consumed is only the fanciful portraits of Life-of-Jesus theology, and that means nothing other than "Christ after the flesh".'[40]

In each case God can be known only in non-theoretical contexts, only ever as the subject, the One in whose presence man stands, never as the object, someone for man to investigate.

To develop and document this tradition would require a large study in itself, yet the point can be illustrated briefly from the case of Schleiermacher. He argues the following theses : Firstly that religion is distinct both from science and morality.

[39] Introduction to *The So-called Historical Jesus and the Historical Biblical Christ*, M. Kahler, trans. C. Braatan (1964).
[40] *Faith and Understanding I*, ed. R. W. Funk (1969), p. 132.

'Religion is not knowledge and science, either of the world or of God. Without being knowledge, it recognizes knowledge and science. In itself it is an affection, a revelation of the Infinite in the finite, God being seen in it and it in God.'[41]

'The piety which forms the basis of all ecclesiastical communions is, considered purely in itself, neither a Knowing nor a Doing, but a modification of Feeling, or of immediate self-consciousness.'[42]

In asserting that religion consists in the feeling of absolute dependence Schleiermacher departs sharply from Kant's own positive view, but in asserting that it is distinct from both science and morality he stays within Kant's epistemological framework.

Secondly, religion is a feeling of absolute dependence. That is, religion and religious belief are analysed in immanentist terms, in terms of feelings.

Thirdly, religious doctrines are the constructs out of reflection on religious feeling. Theology becomes anthropology (and the critique of Feuerbach becomes intelligible).

'Since the feeling of absolute dependence, even in the realm of redemption, only puts in an appearance, i.e. becomes a real self-consciousness in time, in so far as it is aroused by another determination of the self-conscious and unites itself therewith, every formula for that feeling is a formula for a definite state of mind; and consequently all propositions of Dogmatics must be capable of being set up as such formulae . . . Thus conceived, the dogmatic propositions become utterances regarding the constitution of the world, but only for the feeling of absolute dependence and with reference to it.'[43]

So, for Schleiermacher, a believer is one who has a characteristic 'affection', a feeling of absolute dependence, and religious doctrine is simply the reconstruction and systematization of these feelings. As with Kant religious belief is scarcely belief-that, and what makes it religious is not that it gives knowledge of God, but that it expresses certain human states.

[41] *On Religion. Speeches to its Cultured Despisers*, trans. J. Oman (1958), p. 36.
[42] *The Christian Faith*, ed. H. R. Macintosh and J. S. Stewart (1928), p. 5.
[43] op. cit., p. 126.

8

ACQUAINTANCE

John Hick, in a number of writings, notably *Faith and Knowledge*[1], has developed the thesis that religious belief is like knowledge by acquaintance. On this view religious belief is not a case of knowledge by acquaintance but is to be understood on the model of knowledge by acquaintance. The knowledge of God that it is claimed the believer has is not that he sees God but that he has a direct non-sensory but cognitive experience of God which provides not anyone, but the one who has the experience, with the grounds to claim 'I know God'. So that in Hick's view religious belief is a case of ideological knowledge by acquaintance, in the sense that religious faith is based on experiences that not everyone has, though Hick seems to suggest in places that anyone *could* have them.

In discussing Hick's thesis it is necessary to be more critical than in the case of the other models discussed, for the following reason. Although certain important points of the thesis are open to objection, the main difficulty is not that this view is internally incoherent, but that its scope is narrower than Hick believes it to be. That is, if the objections that are to be made are valid ones, they do not show it to be a replacement of other models of belief (as Hick suggests that it is, particularly in the first chapter of *Faith and Knowledge*), but that it is a different model. The grounds for saying this are, briefly, that the necessary religious and theological accompaniments of this view are different from that, say, of religious belief as assent. It is not possible simply to slot in this model of religious belief without disturbing anything else. Hick's view is an entirely different account of faith from the traditional Protestant-Thomist account. It is based on different presuppositions, and so does not, strictly, rival the tradi-

[1] Second Edition (1966).

tional view. If this claim can be upheld, it will be a vindication of the general thesis of this book, that different models of belief operate in religion, and that these models are inextricably intertwined with substantive religious views.

I

This exposition of Hick's view will concentrate on its three essential features : (*a*) that religious knowledge is like the immediate knowledge one person may have of another, (*b*) that it involves an interpretative element, and (*c*) that it is unconstrained. The phrases 'religious knowledge' or 'knowledge of God' are used in preference to 'faith' in order to highlight the epistemology, and to leave the psychological features of religious faith to one side. In looking at Hick's views, his lecture 'Religious Faith as Experiencing-As',[2] as well as *Faith and Knowledge* will be used, because the lecture is in some respects clearer and more fully worked out than the chapter 'The nature of Faith' in the book.

Hick stresses that religious knowledge is something immediate, and that it involves the apprehending of God in the ordinary environment of life. It is 'an awareness of the divine being mediated through awareness of the world, the supernatural through the natural'. This is argued for on the grounds that all experience, including sense-experience, is 'significant' in the way in which Hick wants to say that knowledge of God is significant. That is, sense-perception involves interpretation, or, as he puts it in the lecture, using Wittgenstein's terminology and illustrations, all perception involves 'seeing as'. Similarly with moral situations; seeing (metaphorically) a particular state of affairs as imposing an obligation is attaching significance to some feature of the environment.

'A traveller on an unfrequented road, for example, comes upon a stranger who has met with an accident and who is lying injured and in need of help. At the level of natural significance this is just an empirical state of affairs, a particular configuration of stone and earth and flesh. But an act or reflex of interpretation at the moral level reveals to the traveller a situation in which he is

[2] In *Talk of God*, ed. G. N. A. Vesey (1969).

under obligation to render aid. He feels a categorical imperative laid upon him, demanding that he help the injured man.'[3]

The perceiving of religious significance is at a higher level still, and is a matter of the 'total interpretation' of one's life.

'The monotheist's faith-apprehension of God as the unseen Person dealing with him in and through his experience of the world is from the point of view of epistemology an interpretation of this kind, an interpretation of the world as a whole as mediating a divine presence and purpose. He sees in his situation as a human being a significance to which the appropriate response is a religious trust and obedience'.[4]

Hick explicitly regards this account of religious knowledge as a form of knowledge by acquaintance or 'cognition in presence', to be assimilated not to propositional belief, but to perception. In a paper of fifteen pages he has at least twenty different ways of expressing this. Here are some of them: 'knowing God by faith', 'cognition of God by acquaintance', 'encounters with God', 'personal dealings with the divine Thou', 'cognition of God by faith', 'faith is the awareness of God itself', 'experiencing life as a continual interaction with the transcendent God', 'awareness of existing in the presence of God', 'divine presence borne in upon us', 'contemplative and mystical awareness of God'. All these expressions would appear to be usable more or less interchangeably by Hick, and all stress the immediacy of religious knowledge.

What Hick means by faith being interpretive is that it is to be modelled on seeing-as. As noted, Hick uses 'perception' very widely, to include not just the reception of sense-impressions but also moral and religious attitudes. All such perception, on whatever level – natural, moral or religious – involves interpretation or recognition. Yet while religious significance is at a higher level in the hierarchy than ethical significance

'not every moment of religious awareness is superimposed upon some occasion of moral obligation. Very often – and especially

[3] *Faith and Knowledge*, p. 111.
[4] ibid., pp. 114–5.

in the prophetic type of religion that we know in Judaism and Christianity – the sense of the presence of God does carry with it some specific or general moral demand. But we may also be conscious of God in solitude, surrounded only by the natural world, when the divine presence is borne in upon us by the vastness of the starry heavens above or the majestic beauty of a sunrise or a mountain range or some lake or forest scene, or other aspect of the earth's marvellously varied face. Again, the sense of the presence of God may occur without any specific environmental context, when the mind is wrapt in prayer or meditation; for there is a contemplative and mystical awareness of God which is relatively independent of external circumstances.'[5]

Part of the insistence of Hick on this interpretative character of religious knowledge is his concern to make it free, in the sense of unconstrained. At each level of the perceptual hierarchy there is 'an unavoidable element of personal interpretation'. 'Our knowledge of God, on the view advocated here, is not given to use as a compulsory perception, but is achieved as a voluntary act of interpretation.'[6] While interpretation is required at each level, the extent of 'cognitive freedom' increases at each level of the hierarchy. A necessary condition of the relation between God and man being personal, that is, voluntary and unconstrained, is that God is regarded as *deus absconditus*.

'He must, so to speak, stand back, hiding himself behind his creation, and leaving to us the freedom to recognize or fail to recognize his dealings with us. Therefore God does not manipulate our minds or override our wills, but seeks our unforced recognition of his presence, and our free allegiance to his purposes. He desires, not a compelled obedience, but our uncoerced growth towards the humanity revealed in Christ.'[7]

Two finals points in this sketch of Hick's view ought to be mentioned. First it needs to be stressed, again, that the 'knowledge' that Hick refers to is a knowledge-claim which the claimer believes he has grounds for. The religious man's awareness of 'being

---

[5] *Talk of God*, pp. 30–1.
[6] *Faith and Knowledge*, p. 121.
[7] ibid., p. 135.

in the unseen presence of God' constitutes a sufficient reason *for the religious man himself* to be sure of the reality of God. The religious experience of knowing God described above, though it is not an argument for the existence of God *tout court*, is in Hick's view an argument for the believer's right to claim that he knows God.

The second thing is to discuss the part that propositions play in this account. We saw in Chapter 4 that it is plausible, following Hintikka, to interpret knowledge by acquaintance in terms of directly individuated propositions. However, Hick stresses, in his account of faith as knowledge by acquaintance, both that faith itself is non-propositional, and that propositions arise out of the knowledge by acquaintance. He seems to assume the Russellian point with respect to acquaintance, that 'our knowledge of things is logically independent of our knowledge of truths'. But if the knowledge by acquaintance is not a propositional attitude, but a non-propositional attitude, then the question of the propositional content of the attitude cannot presumably arise, and it becomes hard to see how propositions can play even a secondary role that is non-arbitrary in character. There is nothing propositional for them to be checked against. And how can these propositions, having a secondary role as accounts of religious experience, act as criteria of reidentification if what they reidentify has no propositional content?

We must say, despite the parallels that Hick draws between his own views and those of Martin Buber, that he cannot mean that knowledge by acquaintance is non-propositional, but that he uses the acquaintance model to stress the immediacy of valid religious faith.

Suppose that we take seriously the analogy with knowledge by acquaintance. Then the following problem arises. It makes sense to ask 'Is Smith's acquaintance Jones the same individual as his acquaintance the editor of *The Examiner*?' What would the equivalent question for Hick be? Clearly, if the idea that God is mediated through the whole of experience is taken seriously, there will be no equivalent question. On the other hand, if Hick means that God is mediated by the whole of experience *on a given occasion*, then it would make sense to ask if the idea mediated by the whole of experience on occasion O_1 is the same as that mediated by the whole of experience on a subsequent occasion O_2.

Hick stresses, as we have seen, that the experience is ambiguous. This means, presumably, that it is like having met someone who could be Smith or Jones, where the names stand for different individuals and are not different names of the same individual. That is, there is ambiguity or opacity to the experience in that it is possible for two individuals to experience identical states of affairs and not attribute the same significance to them. A can be acquainted with all that B is acquainted with when B is acquainted with God, and not be acquainted with God, because of this opacity or ambiguity.

Such religious propositions as are found in the Bible or the Creeds (say) are the verbal precipitate of faith, at least insofar as these propositions are regarded as religiously adequate. So Hick writes of the Old Testament that 'the prophets experienced the religious significance of these events and declared it to the people'. That is to say, the prophets perceived certain events as acts of God and gave an account of their experience, insofar as they were able to verbalize it, to the people. Similarly with the Creeds. Hick makes a sharp distinction between what he calls faith *in* Christ and faith *from* Christ. The first consists of 'the basic convictions which directly transcribe Christian experience, providing matter for subsequent theological reflection', the second of 'theological reflection itself and the formulations in which it has issued'.[8] Religious doctrines are theories about religious facts, and religious facts are experiences of God.

II

As stated earlier there are certain incoherences in this account, though not of such a character as to destroy it. After discussing these it will be argued that, quite independently of such incoherences, there are certain facts that make it clear that Hick's account is narrower in scope than he thinks. It is not a rival account to the view of faith as assent; it is another account entirely. The way in which Hick presents his views suggests the conceptual imperialism that has plagued accounts of religious

[8] ibid., p. 218.

K

belief : the setting up of a theory or model and the claim that all religious belief or knowledge is to be understood in this way.

The incoherence concerns the relation between religious knowledge and the will. In the *Investigations* Wittgenstein wrote :

'Seeing an aspect and imagining are subject to the will. There is such an order as "Imagine *this*", and also : "Now see the figure like *this*"; but not "Now see this leaf green".'[9]

Hick argues that faith is like seeing something as something else (seeing a duck as a rabbit), and that such an act of faith is subject to the will, and guarantees 'cognitive freedom'. But on this view how can faith be distinguished from imagination? It is not clear that Hick regards this as a difficulty, because another of the distinctive merits of his view of faith, as he sees it, is that it can be 'integrated into the theistic and anti-theistic world-views respectively'.[10]

The atheist will say that to claim to know God by faith is to invoke an ontological myth, but on the other hand for the theist the 'religious apperception passes through the world to God, seeing the natural as mediating the Supernatural. It entails an ontological claim that has no analogy in the sphere of aesthetics.'[11] Hick wishes to say both (*a*) that this account of faith is 'epistemologically neutral' as between theism and atheism, and (*b*) that for the believer faith differs from imagination. It is hard to see how these two positions can be held consistently. It does not help to say that religious knowledge for the believer makes certain ontological claims, for so, often, does imagination for the imaginer. For example, someone may think that there is a man in the shadows but be imagining it.

It might be said that just as faith or religious knowledge (in Hick's sense) and imagination can be confused, so can religious belief, faith (as propositional assent) and make-believe. But the difference is that in the traditional case there is separate evidence. Someone might consider that the Christian Faith is make-believe,

[9] *Philosophical Investigations* (1953), p. 213e.
[10] *Faith and Knowledge*, p. 144.
[11] ibid., p. 145.

consisting of false or superstitious beliefs, but he has an intellectual right to do this only after considering the appropriate evidence. In the case of Hick's view there is no evidence – other than the seeing-as of religious believers – to consider, and cannot be. For if there were, this would be expressed in propositions, and the religious knowledge that had this evidence for its object would be knowledge by description, and not knowledge by acquaintance.

All that can be said, it seems, is that there is no *communicable* difference between religious knowledge and imagination, (or, if it is insisted that religious knowledge has evidence, that this evidence is not communicible, otherwise it would be descriptive and hence would fall outside this model of religious knowledge). Yet Hick must say that when someone apprehends God he knows that he is not imagining things. Hick might say that faith is distinguishable from imagination by its attitudinal and behavioural effects. But this is not a very strong argument, for religious belief as propositional is distinguishable from imagination by just such effects as well.

A second difficulty has to do with the phrase 'cognitive freedom'. In contrasting sense-perception with knowledge of God, Hick says that whereas 'certain aspects of our environment force themselves upon our attention' other aspects 'can only reach us if we ourselves admit them across our personal frontiers'. He also writes of people having a propensity to interpret life in religious terms, of 'voluntarily recognizing God'[12] and of 'being free to become or refrain from becoming aware of Him'.[13] Before coming to discuss the sense in which our environment may be said to be 'coercive' it is necessary to examine the phrases 'admit . . . across our personal frontiers', 'voluntarily recognize', and 'free to become aware of'.

Each of these phrases, in ordinary English, presupposes what might be called epistemic recognition or identification. That is to say, the objects of such expressions must take certain descriptions. Before a trades union can be recognized before the law, it must exist and be identified. The question 'Is X (the trades union under some description) to be recognized?' must be ask-

[12] ibid., p. 128, 134, 136.
[13] In a note 'Faith and Coercion', *Philosophy*, 1967, p. 273.

able. But Hick understands religious knowledge not as the recognition of someone previously unidentified under a different description but as the recognition of someone previously unidentified until the believer voluntarily recognizes him. It is not that someone can first know of the existence and character of God, and so identify God, and then go on to choose to recognize this God, or to admit him across his personal frontiers.[14]

Hick might claim that this objection is based on a confusion. Though he cannot allow that God can be known by description, he can allow descriptions of experiences of knowing God. These descriptions might be said to form a tradition, and, Hick might argue, it is by allowing the tradition to give him certain clues that an individual 'masters the technique'. Someone might know of God, and go on to know God.

But there is a further source of difficulty. It is that in the case of seeing-as or experiencing-as at the highest level of the hierarchy (religious seeing-as) there is no feature or features of our environment invariably and uniformly correlated with 'knowing God by faith'. This is because, for Hick, religious knowledge is an act of 'total interpretation', and is not concerned with the identification and recognition of a certain range of particulars. That is to say, there are no data that religious seeing-as is uniformly the seeing-as *of*, as there is in the case of seeing-as at the two lower levels. So there are no publicly identifiable cues for the private, immediate and incommunicable experience that for Hick is religious knowledge. And even were there to be something identifiable as the correlate of religious faith, this would not be seen as divine[15] but seen-as mediating the divine.

It is true that in certain places Hick understands 'cognitive freedom' in a weaker sense, as 'the freedom to encourage or thwart' a 'propensity to construe the world religiously'.[16] The

<hr/>

[14] This seems to be Hick's general position. But writing of the epistemologically-neutral character of faith as seeing-as he says 'It is to be observed that we are not inquiring whether there is any such thing as knowledge of God; in order for there to be agreement about this there would first have to be agreement as to whether there is a God to be the object of such knowledge' (*Faith and Knowledge*, p. 210). This suggests that to know God involves both (a) knowing that there is a God and (b) experiencing life as a dialogue with God.

[15] With the possible exception of Jesus Christ.

[16] *Faith and Knowledge*, p. 139.

remarks that he makes about this are general remarks about propensities, not particular remarks about propensities to construe the world religiously. Party-workers may have a propensity to believe their own propaganda and this propensity can be thwarted or encouraged, and the propensity that men have to 'interpret the data of sensation in terms of our familiar world' can be thwarted or encouraged. If having such propensities was all that Hick meant by 'cognitive freedom' it would create no special epistemological difficulties for his account of religious knowledge, but it is clear that he means more.

This is connected with the idea that seeing x as y requires one to have 'mastered the technique'. That is, it is not possible to see *this* as the apex of the triangle, and then *that*, unless it is known what it is for a triangle to have an apex. But when someone claims to have seen an event as an act of God in the sense that it 'mediates the divine presence' what technique has been mastered?

In Hick's contrast between the unambiguous character of sense-perception and the ambiguous character of our perception of God it seems that two different ideas are being confused together, and that because of this the need for a special account of cognitive freedom (some of the features of which have been examined above) has been misconceived. On this point Hick has written :

'The extent of our cognitive freedom varies in respect of the different aspects of our environment. It is at a minimum in sense perception, and for that reason passes unnoticed by the man in the street. For in perceiving the material world, the physical pole of cognition has become so fully developed in all of us, as the result of a long process of evolution, that it is stable as between mind and mind. Hence as animal organisms we all perceive the same world – that is to say, our several experience-histories are capable of being correlated in terms of hypothetical universal experience. At this level of experience we are – broadly speaking, and with occasional lapses – compelled to experience correctly.'[17]

[17] ibid., p. 123.

To get clear on this it is necessary to distinguish between the physical properties of the external world with which men have to 'reckon', and the beliefs they may or may not hold about the external world. It is because of the physical properties of the world that human beings cannot walk through brick walls, no matter what they believe about brick walls, or how they characterize them. What *is* compulsory about the physical environment is the fact that if men are to survive in it, they must reckon with it in certain ways. But 'reckon with' here is to be understood purely extensionally. It is something that purely physical organisms do, whether or not, in addition to certain physical properties and capacities, they possess minds. If x has to be reckoned with by a person then it has to be reckoned with by anything animate. If a brick wall will stop a man it will also stop a dog. But what concepts physical organisms use in thinking and speaking about their environment (if in fact they do think and speak about it), are not compelled or dictated in the same way as their behaviour. Whether an organism judges that there is food in front of it or not will depend on whether it is a language-user and how developed its language is. But whether it is a language-user or not it will have to 'reckon with' the food if it is to survive.

Hick makes the point that in person-to-person relations no one can be compelled to believe anything. But unless a very crude behaviouristic account of belief is being used, this is surely a general point about belief, not a point about person-to-person belief. No one can be compelled to believe anything – not in the sense that anyone can believe what he likes about anything but in the sense that a person is free to ignore the grounds for any belief. Because of this, every bit of evidence presented to the mind (as opposed, perhaps, to evidence presented to the senses) may be said to be ambiguous, and to involve the will. Not, again, because it is possible to choose to believe p, just like that, or if we know that p, choose not to know that p, but in the sense that it is possible to choose whether or not to listen to testimony, to follow arguments, or to accept evidence. That is, it is possible, if people choose, to ignore beliefs or knowledge-claims and their grounds.

If this is right, if it is the case that no one can be compelled to believe p, where p is a proposition about some physical fact of the environment (e.g. the proposition 'There is a piece of bread and butter in front of me') then they are free to believe the proposition 'It is not the case that there is a piece of bread and butter in front of me', even though before long the object in front might have to be 'reckoned with', that is, eaten. If men are free to believe p or not-p then (in Hick's sense of the word) p is ambiguous, (or contains terms that are ambiguous). If this is true of all *beliefs*, as against all those matters which organisms have to *reckon with*, then every piece of evidence presented to the mind is ambiguous in this sense. So that the sharp contrast made by Hick between coercion and non-coercion is not one that can be drawn between certain beliefs and others. It is irrelevant to his argument about the features of *religious* as against other sorts of belief. That Hick has not seen this may be due in part to the ambiguity of 'experience', a word which plays a large part in his account. 'Experience' may be epistemic, or merely sensory.

This claim of Hick's about the ambiguity of certain levels of experience is necessary because of his fear that, if it were not ambiguous, obedience to God would be compelled obedience. Because obedience to God must not be compelled, knowledge of God must be free and voluntary, and for knowledge of God to be free and voluntary the evidence for God must be ambiguous. So far it has been argued that the idea of cognitive freedom has difficulties, and that the contrast between ambiguous and unambiguous beliefs or experiences does not exist. It is necessary now to say something about the idea of compelled obedience.

Two things can be granted at once. First, that the evidence for God is not necessarily coercive; God is not a physical entity with which we have to reckon if we are to survive as physical organisms. Earthworms do not reckon with God, and they survive. Secondly, let it be granted, as Hick says, that God does not 'desire a compelled obedience'[18] if by this is meant obedience brought about solely through fear of punishment, for example. But it is not the case that the only alternative to such a view is that a person is free to become aware of God or not, as he chooses, even granting that the idea of being free to become aware of God or not is intelligible. Another alternative is to

[18] ibid., p. 135.

believe in God, and to obey God because it is thought there are good grounds for believing in and obeying him. And if someone has good grounds for obeying God (as he thinks) this need not imply that this obedience is compelled either in the sense that it is heteronomous or that it is accompanied by feelings of compulsion or constraint. Whether such feelings are present or not is contingent upon such factors as whether or not the person is disinclined to obey, and so forth. It would seem that what is at the back of Hick's remarks at this point is what has been referred to as a contra-causal view of freedom as being necessary for responsibility,[19] but to follow this through would take us too far afield.

There is one rather odd aspect to Hick's remarks on compulsion. At one point in *Faith and Knowledge* he writes

'We are focusing attention instead upon the question whether it is proper for the man who reports a compelling awareness of God to *claim* to know that God exists . . . It seems that a sufficiently vivid religious experience would entitle a man to claim to know that God is real. Indeed if his sense of the divine presence is sufficiently powerful he can hardly fail to make this claim. He is sure that God exists, and in his own experience of the presence of God he has a good, and compelling, reason to be sure of it.'[20]

What is meant by 'compelling awareness' and 'compelling reason' here? Presumably an awareness of x is compelling if the perceiver is compelled to recognize x as x. But, as Hick has argued, being compelled to recognize an act as mediating the presence of God is incompatible with cognitive freedom, so that these words at first sight seem to contradict the main claims made by Hick that God never compels knowledge of himself. Perhaps the reply would be that this is the case of a man who has not thwarted his propensity to interpret the world religiously, and has reached the point where he is compelled. But then, presumably, at any time it is open to him to choose not to be compelled, since faith is like seeing-as, and seeing-as is subject to the will.

---

[19] Part of Hick's Irenaean theodicy in *Evil and the God of Love* (1966).
[20] *Faith and Knowledge*, p. 210.

It was noted earlier that one important aspect of Hick's account is that in his view it makes possible human autonomy and an account of the relation between man and God in fully personal terms. Whether he thinks that *only* his view of religious knowledge makes this possible is not clear, but he certainly seems to imply that the idea of faith as propositional belief makes it impossible. Before turning to make some remarks on the scope of Hicks' model it is worth noting that, understood as knowledge by description, religious belief has fewer difficulties in this area of the relation between faith and the will than Hick's account.

If religious belief is regarded as a case of knowledge by description there is no more danger of religious belief being mistaken for imagination than there is for belief being so mistaken. It may be said to be mistaken or superstitious belief because of the inadequacy of the grounds of the belief, or the notions it employs, and as a consequence religious believers may be said to be 'imagining things'. But this is simply a colourful way of saying that their beliefs are false.

In the sense in which Hick wants religious faith to be uncompelled (in so far as this sense can be made clear), all beliefs are subject to the will. H. H. Price has remarked that 'You cannot help preferring the proposition which your evidence favours'.[21] But the 'cannot' here is not a case of 'cannot, whether I like it or not' as it is in 'I cannot help biting my fingernails'. The only alternative to this seems to be a view of the will as causally indeterminate, which brings its own problems. Hick sets some store by the fact that his account is acceptable to both theist and atheist. But then so is the idea of religious belief as belief in certain propositions. On this account the difference between theist and atheist is that the atheist has good reason (as he thinks) for regarding the propositions of religion as meaningless or false, whereas the believer regards them as meaningful and either probably or certainly true. Finally, on the view of religious belief as propositional, it is possible to answer the objection against Hick's account that seeing an event as an act of God requires one to have the notion of an act of God, i.e. to have the notion of a 'neat', unmediated act of God. For on the account of religious

---

[21] 'Belief and Will' in *Philosophy of Mind*, ed. Hampshire (1966), p. 106.

belief as propositional, to see an act as an act of God is just a different way of saying that one believes some act or event to be an act of God, and what is required to make this good is evidence.

III

It was shown earlier that Hick offers the thesis of *Faith and Knowledge* as a better account of religious knowledge than that offered by the view of religious belief as consisting simply in belief in certain propositions. But there is reason to think that the ground it covers is less than and different from that covered by the view of faith as a propositional attitude. His view does not in fact rival this, and requires a different account of religion as well. The grounds for this conclusion are that the range of expressions used by Hick to characterize 'knowledge of God' makes it impossible to give a single account of them. It is possible to discern three varieties at least, which will be referred to as (*a*) evidential beliefs, (*b*) direct experiences or 'encounters', and (*c*) complementary beliefs. By direct experiences or 'encounters' is meant those experiences in which people take themselves to be in direct communion with God. 'Mystical' might be a better word, except that it has come to mean almost anything.

When Hick writes of faith as a person's 'religious response to God's redemptive action in the life of Jesus of Nazareth', such a response has a propositional basis identifiable independently of the response. What the person responds to is a *report about* Jesus of Nazareth, and it is necessary for the person who responds in this way to believe such propositions as 'Jesus of Nazareth existed', and many more besides. So that on this characterization of faith it is a straightforward propositional belief.

When, on the other hand, Hick writes of experiencing an act as an act of God,[22] no evidence other than the awareness of the act is required for this to be a case of religious faith, and such questions as 'Why do you experience this event as an act of God and not this other event?' become relevant, and perhaps awkward, questions to answer. And when he describes faith as an encounter with God, or as a case of being conscious of God or

---

[22] 'Religious Faith as experiencing-as', p. 26.

aware of God, this seems to be a direct experience in that it does not supervene on another non-religious act. In direct experiences no action or event is being interpreted, and the experience takes place independently of any particular action or event. It is true that Hick does at one point[23] differentiate between a contemplative and mystical awareness of God and 'the prophetic type of religious experience', but not on the grounds that these are two different kinds of experience : only that the former may have a looser link with ethics than the latter.

'Thus the dispositional response which is part of the awareness of God is a response in terms of our involvement with our neighbours within our common environment. Even the awareness of God through nature and mystical contemplation leads eventually back to the service of God in the world.'[24]

This bracketing together of a religious response to Jesus and an awareness of God that includes mystical experiences is misleading. While the first is mediated by separately identifiable events, knowable by description, the second is not. Hick says of direct experiences 'the sense of the presence of God may occur without any specific environmental context, when the mind is wrapt in prayer or mediation'. But in this case what is it that is perceived-as or experienced-as? This is an experience that is personal, interior, and not dependent on events which in themselves (according to Hick) are ambiguous but which may be taken to be divine acts.

But there is a more fundamental reason why it is misleading to conflate these cases. 'Having a sense of the presence of God', 'being aware of God', 'having an encounter with God' – these are expressions that can only be used to characterize episodes. It would seem to be a necessary truth about mystical experiences that they are episodic – they are conscious experiences, lasting for so long. It makes sense to ask when they began and when they ended, and so forth.

But this is not true of the third class of expressions that Hick uses to characterize faith or religious knowledge – what were referred to above as complementary beliefs e.g. 'experiencing life

---

[23] ibid., pp. 30–1.
[24] ibid., p. 31.

as a continual interaction with the transcendent God', 'life as a sphere in which we have continually to do with God and he with us'. 'Regarding the whole of one's life as involving dealings with God', 'living one's life as a religious response to God' – these are dispositional expressions, and do not seem to involve the having of particular experiences which one takes to be of God. A man's whole life can be a religious response to God, and he can be said to regard his life as a religious response to God when his mind is occupied with all sorts of extraneous things, but a man cannot have a direct experience of God when his mind is so occupied.

It ought to be stressed at this point that our concern is only with questions of classification. Whether men do have such experiences, or are justified in having such beliefs as we have tried to classify above, is a different question.

It has been suggested that Hick has thrown together cases that ought to be kept separate. This can be supported by considering particular examples. Though Hick's model of religious knowledge as cognition-in-presence *might* work for certain cases it is not appropriate as a model for religious belief as it operates in a historically-grounded religion such as Christianity. (By 'historically-grounded religion' is simply meant one whose distinctive character depends on the truth of certain historical claims.) People do, as Hick says, claim to see the presence of God mediated by the world around them. But what about the particular historical claims of a religion such as Christianity?

Many religious believers, including theologians particularly in the post-Kantian tradition, wish to say that the truth of the historical claims of a religion such as Christianity is not required for the value of the Christian religion. The religion is logically independent of the facts. This is a possible position. But it would be too much to say it was the only possible position. While some religious believers are willing to let the historical data go as unimportant, others regard it is crucial. There are many models of religious belief.

It is open to Hick to reject the idea of religious belief that regards history as crucial. But the price that must be paid for this is to allow that his model of religious belief or religious knowledge does not cover such cases.

It was mentioned earlier that at one point Hick speaks of faith as 'a religious response to God's redemptive action in Christ'.[25] The claim of Christianity, as traditionally understood, is that this action took place in history, as Hick himself says, 'in the life of Jesus of Nazareth'. But if this is so, then, barring miracles, no one can know the events of the life of Jesus of Nazareth other than by description. It is clear that Hick wishes to recognize the revelatory character of Jesus, but how is he going to be able to do this consistently with his own account of religious knowledge? How is it possible to hold both (a) that faith is like perception in that it is a case of cognition in presence, and (b) that faith is a religious response to a person who lived many years ago? In the second case what is the cognition in presence cognition of? In the case of seeing the events of one's life as an encounter with God one is in the presence of material objects, one sees events etc. But in the other case one is only in the presence of a set of propositions about a certain unique historical figure.

The same problem can be put in the form of a query about Hick's use of the term 'revelatory'. In the closing section of his Royal Institute lecture he distinguishes between primary and secondary senses of the word. The Bible is revelatory in a primary sense because it contains events of unique significance 'which became revelatory through the faith of the biblical writers'. It is revelatory in a secondary sense because it mediates to subsequent generations the same revelation 'calling in its own turn for a response of faith'.[26] What is the relation between these two senses of 'revelatory'? The one requires knowledge by acquaintance, the other knowledge by description.

Part of the reason for this difficulty is that Hick wishes on the one hand to stress the immediacy of religious faith (hence the assimilation of it to perception), and on the other hand he is working with a particular model, adapted from Wittgenstein, of perception as being epistemic, as entailing recognition or identification. Now it may be the case that the notion of perception entails the notion of recognition, and Hick may be saying this by his claim that all perception is perception-as, though he does not say whether this is a necessary or contingent fact about perception. However this may be it is certain that there is no reverse implication. Recognizing or identifying x as such and such does not imply that x is known by acquaintance. The class of cases of knowledge by acquaintance is not identical with the class of cases of identification-as such and such (even supposing that perception entails identification). This can be shown by considering that a narrative, something necessarily known by description, can be interpreted in a particular way, can be seen-as a story of a certain sort. It can be seen-as symbolic, or as pointing to a moral, say. Or the characters portrayed in the story can be recognized to be timid or avaricious, without us knowing any of them by acquaintance. Indeed it may be logically impossible to know the characters by acquaintance if the story is fictional.

The point of the duck-rabbit example in the *Investigations* is to make the distinction between seeing and what Wittgenstein called 'noticing an aspect'. What a person sees may not change and yet he may notice first one aspect of what he sees, then another. The characteristics of a drawing remain the same while the significance of it can change according as one directs one's attention. As Hick shows (in the case of what earlier is referred to as a complementary belief), a religious belief can supervene on ordinary beliefs in the following way: the believer and unbeliever are agreed on 'the facts', but disagree on the significance of them. One sees a particular act as an act of God's providence, another does not. The Pharisees and Romans may not have seen Jesus of Nazareth as the Christ, but the disciples of Jesus did. Each is exposed to the same selection of data, but each takes what he sees differently. This can happen, but it is not all that can happen. There can be very different cases.

Suppose someone claims to see the resurrection of Jesus as an act of God. What is involved in this? A necessary condition of seeing the resurrection of Jesus as an act of God, or as revelatory of God, or as anything, is that (at least) it is believed that the resurrection of Jesus took place. In connection with miracles Hick says 'we may say that a miracle is any event that is experienced as a miracle'. This is not circular because Hick defines a miracle as an event that is religiously significant.

'A miracle, whatever else it may be, is an event through which we become vividly and immediately conscious of God as acting towards us. A startling happening, even if it should involve a suspension of natural law, does not constitute for us a miracle in the religious sense of the word if it fails to make us intensely aware of being in God's presence. In order to be miraculous, an event must be experienced as religiously significant.'[27]

It seems from this that what is necessary and sufficient for an event's being a miracle is that it has a certain religious significance. But this does not help to answer the question. Hick wants to say that seeing an event as religiously significant is like seeing a duck as a rabbit, or (perhaps) like seeing a configuration of chalk as a rabbit. But this analogy does not hold, for in the case of seeing an event such as a resurrection as religiously significant there is no neutral description of the event that is acceptable to both believer and unbeliever. The difference is not necessarily that both believe in the (metaphysical) miracle, the resurrection, but that one denies, while the other asserts, that the resurrection was also a religious miracle. There may be a difference over the evidence.

The point may be put as follows. There can be at least three sorts of scepticism in a religion such as Christianity which has a historical base and is not simply a 'natural' religion such as deism. First, ontological scepticism, scepticism about the existence of God, for example. Secondly, scepticism about the evidence for particular historical claims required by some as essential to the religion, such as the virgin birth of Christ, or the miracles he performed. This scepticism could be on either *a priori* or *a posteriori* grounds. Finally, scepticism about the significance of the evidence. These sorts of scepticism are related, in that scepticism about the first entails scepticism about the second and third, scepticism about the second entails scepticism about the third. That is, the question of the evidence for Christianity cannot meaningfully be raised without the existence of God either being presupposed or established in some way, and questions about the significance of the evidence cannot be raised until the evidence has been established in some way.

If the claim is made by religious believers that God is revealed

[27] ibid., pp. 34–5.

through a particular suspension of physical laws, it is possible (granting the existence of God) either to deny that the suspension did in fact take place, or allow that in this case a law of nature was suspended but deny that it has a miraculous character, explaining it as a statistical freak or something.

While the analogy Hick draws between the duck-rabbit and seeing events as revelatory of God may do where there are those who are prepared to allow that a miracle has taken place *if* they can be shown its significance, it will not do for those cases where there is a dispute between believer and unbeliever over the evidence, as has happened classically in the case of Christianity. Here there is a more basic disagreement, one that affects the *description* of the data for which a certain significance is claimed. The shape on the black-board must be agreed *before* the question of whether it is a duck-like or rabbit-like shape can be discussed. When Hick says 'there is a sense in which the religious man and the atheist both live in the same world and another sense in which they live consciously in different worlds', this may be true in the case of events taking place today, but it is not true of events that (it is claimed by some) took place years ago in Palestine. The difference between believer and unbeliever is not merely at the level of perceiving a certain event as an act of God but of affirming or denying that such an event took place. And so the difference between them cannot be expressed as a difference in the significance to be attached to events. For the atheist, or the sceptic about the historical claims of Christianity, there is no event for significance to be attached to, only a set of hallucinations.

Before one can begin to apply a hierarchy of concepts to a thing, before someone can be taught to regard the thing not only as a speck in the sky but as a bird, not only as a bird but as a hawk, it must be possible to identify what is being denoted independently of the higher-level ways of denoting it. But this is just what is not possible in the case of some disputes between sceptics and believers. Recognizing or identifying something as such and such may require one to go beyond what is presented to the senses but one cannot be released from what is presented to the senses. Though it may in practice be difficult to establish just when recognition ends and imagination begins, it is perfectly obvious that a plain spherical shape cannot be 'seen as' a battleship.

In expounding Hick's view of religious knowledge, two lines of criticism have been developed : that his view has certain internal incoherences, particularly in what he says about religious belief or religious knowledge and the will, and, secondly, that his model is of a narrower scope than he maintains in his writings. There are three different cases, at least, covered by what he calls knowledge of God or religious knowledge – 'direct' experiences of God; responses to particular historical beliefs; and religious beliefs about one's own and other's lives. Hick's model of knowledge may do for the first and the third of these, if the incoherences can be overcome, but not for the second. Again, it should be stressed that it is open to Hick and to anyone else to argue that one or other of these cases is religiously unimportant, though it is hard to see on what grounds this could be done without begging vital questions.

IV

Hick's account is thus not a rival to propositional accounts of religious belief, i.e. those that regard religious belief as a case of believing either probably true or certainly true propositions. It covers a different area from this view, and is a different theory. In this closing section these claims are developed briefly.

Hick's view implies a different account of the object of religious knowledge or belief from that in the propositional accounts discussed in Chapters 5 and 6. 'Revelation' is simply a set of privileged accounts of men who have in the past seen events etc. as acts of God. It has the logical form of a record of encounters, not of (as in classical views of Christianity) a message from God to be accepted. Because of this Hick speaks of religious knowledge rather than of religious belief, because the object of belief is not a set of propositions (however validated and made credit-worthy) but God himself. It is clear that, since Hick has such a different account of revelation, other theological differences are likely, but these fall outside the scope of this study. Secondly, the act of belief and the object of belief, separate on the propositional accounts of religious belief, are merged on Hick's model. The grounds of religious belief or knowledge become part of the act of believing or knowing, so that it is impossible

L

to specify the grounds independently of the faith that perceives them. The description of what is believed or known is necessarily the description from the point of view of the believer or knower. So that the object of faith or knowledge can never be identified as a set of assertions, promises or whatever with a given meaning, which the believer accepts and the unbeliever rejects. Given that Hick's account is to be restricted in the way suggested above, this is not incoherent, but if not, he is left open to the charge of subjectivism. Whether he is right in thinking that only his model of religious knowledge does justice to what he calls the immediacy of religious experience is something that is discussed elsewhere in this study.

Put more formally, Hick's view is as follows :

An individual I has faith in/knows (Hick uses these interchangeably) God if and only if he voluntarily chooses to interpret a particular event or act, or a set of events or acts, or the whole of his life, as mediating the presence of God.

This model has three important implications, mentioned here, and discussed more fully in the final chapter. It is not simply a subjective account of religious knowledge or belief, or at least Hick has arguments against understanding his view in this way. Knowledge of God is not a *blik* but something that can be regarded as veridical or illusory. Claiming to know God makes a difference to the believer, not simply in the sense that it changes him ('integrates' him, provides him with motivation or whatever), but in the sense that his faith gives rise to expectations that are verifiable or falsifiable in the future. Hence the stress by Hick on 'eschatological verification'. If what Hick says about knowledge being interpretative is true, then even in the *eschaton* the individual unbeliever will be free to see these events as something different from the believer. Hick allows this, but seems to think that as a matter of fact they will not.

'If this be so, it has the consequence that only the theistic believer can find the vindication of his belief. This circumstance would not of course set any restriction upon who can become a believer, but it would entail that while theistic faith can be verified – found by one who holds it to be beyond rational doubt – yet it cannot be proved to the nonbeliever. Such an asymmetry would connect with that strand of New Testament teaching which speaks of a division of mankind even in the world to come.

'Having noted this possibility I will only express my personal opinion that the logic of the New Testament as a whole, though admittedly not always its explicit content, leads to a belief in ultimate universal salvation.'[28]

It is not necessary to go into the notion of eschatological verification which has already been widely discussed in the literature, except to say that, since for Hick religious knowledge involves an act of total interpretation, the verification or falsification of religious claims cannot be something that goes on *within* the universe.[29]

On this understanding of belief there is a certain amount of difficulty in giving an account of disbelief or unbelief. It would appear from the use that Hick makes of the notion of seeing-as or significance, that the difference between unbelief and belief is that believers see the world differently from unbelievers. (That is, it is *as if* the two saw the world differently, for Hick is not saying that they literally see things differently, only that faith is like seeing things differently.) If there is to be symmetry between belief and unbelief then unbelief must be understood as a voluntary choice *not* to see things, or the whole of life as mediating the presence of God. Apart from the difficulties raised by this, parallel to the one raised earlier about belief and the will there is the suggestion in Hick's remarks that to understand a religious claim, and to claim to know God, are two ways of saying the same thing. Because of the assimilation of the grounds of believing and knowing to their acts there seems to be no gap in his account for the case of someone who understands but does not believe. The connection of belief and understanding is the topic of the last chapter, and this difficulty, if it is a difficulty, will be discussed more fully there.

What is the logical status of the knowledge that Hick claims that the religious person has? Hick makes two or three quite separate, and not altogether consistent, points about this. The

---

[28] *Faith and Knowledge*, p. 192–3. This is more fully worked out in *Evil and the God of Love*.

[29] *Faith and Knowledge*, p. 178.

first thing is that, subjectively speaking, there can be certainty for the religious person. That Jones knows God entails that it is possible for Jones to feel certain that he knows God.[30] Secondly, considered as a knowledge-claim it is justifiable for the religious person himself, being based on the evidence of his own experience. But this does not mean, as Hick allows, that Jones's experiences are sufficient evidence for Smith to claim that he (Smith) knows God. So that the knowledge concerned is (in the sense outlined in Chapter 4) ideological knowledge, but ideological knowledge by acquaintance, not by description. Unlike the claims made by the believer in a self-authenticating authority, the claim to know God is not certain, for, according to Hick, no claims to knowledge can be known to be certain. That is, the knowledge-claim is both epistemologically and logically corrigible.[31] But this seems to be contradicted by a remark Hick makes earlier in *Faith and Knowledge* when discussing eschatological verification.

'It is not, then, being suggested that the existence of God has the status in the believer's mind of a tentatively held hypothesis which awaits verification after death. The believer can already have, on the basis of his religious experience, a warrant as to the reality of God. He may already know God in a way which requires no further verification.'[32]

This seems to imply that the believer *knows for certain* that God exists, because he knows God. But presumably this remark must be qualified by the further discussion in which Hick clarifies the notion of certainty. Hick would appear to be saying that the believer can claim to have genuine knowledge of God insofar as he is warranted in claiming that he has knowledge of anything, but with the added qualification that the grounds for knowledge of God are not coercive in the way in which grounds for knowing about material objects are.

[30] ibid., p. 195.
[31] ibid., p. 208–9.
[32] ibid., p. 194.

PART III

9

BELIEF, MEANING AND UNDERSTANDING

In the last Part the attempt was made to distinguish between different concepts of belief as these operate within religion, and to show how these conceptual differences are connected, in each case, with substantive religious positions. In this final Part the importance of these conceptual differences will be underlined by showing how they bear on the much-discussed issues of meaning and understanding in religion.

Four concepts of religious belief have been distinguished:

(*a*) Belief as a judgement of probability, based on certain natural analogies or empirical data.

(*b*) Belief as certainty grounded in the self-authenticating character of a document.

(*c*) Belief as a regulative, moral principle.

(*d*) Belief as an immediate awareness of God, akin to knowledge by acquaintance of persons and material objects.

After some preliminary distinctions have been made, attention will be paid to how 'believers' in each of these senses are committed to responding to Antony Flew's well-known 'falsificationist challenge':

'Just what would have to happen not merely (morally and wrongly) to tempt but also (logically and rightly) to entitle us to say "God does not love us" or even "God does not exist"? I therefore put to the succeeding symposiasts the simple central questions, "What would have to occur or to have occurred to constitute for you a disproof of the love of, or the existence of, God?" '[1]

---

[1] *New Essays in Philosophical Theology*, ed. A. Flew and A. C. MacIntyre (1955), p. 99.

This challenge is capable of being understood in a number of different ways. It might be equivalent to any of the following four questions :

(*a*) What difference does A's belief that p make to him? It is true that this is not a direct gloss on the question above. But it is an implication of some of Flew's remarks – for example, of the question 'What is this assurance of God's (appropriately qualified) love worth?' – that A's belief in God makes *no* difference to him. This question concerns the meaningfulness or point of religious utterances.

(*b*) What would make A change his mind about the truth of p (where p is either 'God exists' or 'God is love')? The implication of Flew's remarks is that nothing would make the believer change his mind, but that he will maintain his belief no matter what comes to pass.

(*c*) What would falsify p? Here the focus is on the evidence that would tend to the disproving of the proposition, not the factors that would tend to the disbelieving of p. This important distinction has, it seems, often been overlooked by those who have debated the falsification issue. Its significance will be discussed below. The implication of Flew's question is that no evidence would tend to disprove the proposition, and so, given his theory of meaning, that the proposition would be meaningless.

(*d*) What reasons would induce A to change his mind as to the truth of p? The implication of Flew's remarks is that no reasons would, (and hence that the belief is irrational).

It is quite possible to side-step the falsification issue by arguing that it is based on an unsatisfactory theory of meaning, as Heimbeck[2] and Plantinga[3] do. It is not an implication of the discussion that follows that particular religious statements are cognitively meaningless if they do not meet the Flew challenge in some way. What it is not possible to do, if the previous discussion of the various notions of religious belief is anything like correct, is to respond to Flew's question by making a simple appeal to 'use' or to the language-game of religion, for there is not one agreed use, and there are many language-games. Our study has

[2] *Theology and Meaning* (1969).
[3] *God and Other Minds* (1967).

tended to confirm the idea of Wittgenstein's, reported by Moore, that in religion there are diverse grammars.[4] The concern here is not with the theory of meaning as applied to religious utterances as such, and so the inadequacies of Flew's question from this point of view are beside the point. Rather the aim now is to show that the various models of belief previously distinguished respond differently to the challenge, and that this fact brings out the differing logical character of these models more sharply.

I

The discussion that follows concentrates on questions (c) and (d) in particular, but a brief comment about the first two is necessary. People find religion pointless because it makes no difference to them. They cannot see what difference believing religious utterances makes. But this is not peculiar to religion. Belief in the divine right of kings can be dismissed as irrelevant, and so meaningless, because believing in it can make no difference to the life of the believer under present conditions.

The second question is of no obvious philosophical relevance, for it refers to the psychological or other causal conditions that may bring about a change in belief, and of course it is quite possible to specify these. Religious belief is not different from other beliefs in being invulnerable to the techniques of brain-washing or indoctrination. The third and fourth questions are the interesting ones as far as the meaning of religious utterances is concerned.

What would falsify A's belief that p? For Kant, because p is not an item of knowledge, but religious belief is practical and wholly regulative, nothing would falsify A's religious belief in God. This is logically parallel to Kant's ethics. Empirical consequences are irrelevant to the obligatoriness of an action, for a sharp contrast is made between doing one's duty, and acting to bring about certain empirically-identifiable consequences. No consequences would stop the rational man telling the truth, and no consequences would stop the rational man believing in God. Belief in God, like the claim of the categorical imperative, is unshakeable.

[4] *Philosophical Papers* (1959), p. 312.

In his study *The Concept of Prayer*[5] which we have already shown to have affinities to Kant's philosophy of religion, D. Z. Phillips makes the point that to look for consequences to justify the ways of God to men is to think anthropomorphically of God and to convict God of the terrible wickedness of bringing about certain acts for certain ends, for example, inoperable cancer for a greater good. There is a clear connection between this and Kantian moral doctrine. For Phillips, the believer's trust in God and thanksgiving to God in no ways depend on the way the world is, or is going. So that to ask 'What would falsify your trust in God?' is a senseless question which misconstrues the grammar of religion. It is a question that does not touch this notion of belief. The thanksgiving is not a thanksgiving *for* certain particulars, or a thanksgiving that certain other particular states have not come about. To thank God for particulars would be to conceive of him anthropomorphically. It would be an example of a natural, not a supernatural belief.

'By thanksgiving, the believer recognizes that life has hope; he is recued from despair, from the feeling of hopelessness. To despair is not to think that *this* or *that* is hopeless, but to think that life itself is hopeless. To see the world as God's creation is to see meaning in life. This meaningfulness remains untouched by the evil in the world because it is not arrived at by an inference from it.'[6]

Phillips's use of words such as 'hope' (which is not hope *for* anything) and 'thanksgiving' obviously demands much more analysis, but the point here is that if predicates of God – such as goodness – are not inferred from the character of the world, after the manner of the argument from design, and if the fact of God's being good makes no difference to the course of events in the world, then God's goodness is not vulnerable to any evidence. On this view of the matter Flew's question reveals a deep misunderstanding of the grammar of religion by conceiving of it as a sort of policy for the future.

Yet in places Phillips does refer to the truth-conditions for religious belief, and this seems to go flatly against Kantianism.

[5] See also 'Religious Beliefs and Language-Games', *Ratio* XII (1970). Reprinted in D. Z. Phillips *Faith and Philosophical Enquiry* (1970).

[6] *The Concept of Prayer*, pp. 97–8.

In *Death and Immortality* he says that belief in immortality has nothing to do with empirical verification[7] but that it is not thereby robbed of its significance. Yet the truth-conditions of the religious 'picture' (Phillips also uses the words 'myth' and 'vision') of immortality are not any set of truths, empirical or otherwise. What are they then? Phillips wishes to say that the 'picture' of immortality is 'true' if, and only if, it provides a reason or in some other way brings it about that the believer, confronted with the picture, believes that he should conduct himself in certain ways. The 'picture' is true in the rather rarified sense of being apt or fertile, a picture of such power that the believer's life is nourished by it. It is in some such way that Phillips holds that the pictures constitute truths.[8]

So that the sense in which religious beliefs are 'true' is pretty Kant-like after all. Religious doctrines regarded as pictures are ways of holding values. They are religious in the sense that they are 'transcendent', not being based on any state of the world, and so are not vulnerable in principle to a verificationist attack. But the religious pictures are not dispensable; they are not simply causal psychological aids to living a certain sort of life, as Braithwaite envisaged parables to function. It is impossible to have other pictures substituted for them.

The response of the Locke-Butler model of belief is altogether different. 'Belief' here is on all fours with belief in non-religious contexts. It is proportioned to evidence, and is logically hypothetical. Hence it is open to falsification. The knowledge that God is supposed to reveal about himself and his ways in 'scripture history' is open to rejection if it can be shown that the history is not to be trusted, on either *a priori* or *a posteriori* grounds (usually the latter, as the claim of this position is that there is nothing *a priori* impossible about miracles). The knowledge of God's character derived from nature is falsifiable (in principle) in a parallel way.

[7] *Death and Immortality*, p. 61. The fact that Peter Winch attributes non-falsifiable religious beliefs to the Azande, while Alasdair MacIntyre regards falsifiability as a necessary condition of any rationally held belief, helps to resolve the conflict between them about 'rationality' and 'relativism'. (See Alasdair MacIntyre, 'Is Understanding Region compatible with Believing?' in *Faith and the Philosophers*, ed. J. Hick (1964), and Peter Winch, 'Understanding a Primitive Society', *American Philosophical Quarterly* (1964).

[8] *Death and Immortality*, p. 71.

The *religious* differences entailed by each of these two models are worth noticing. Though Locke says that the certainty of belief is practically the same as that of knowledge, theoretically they are very different. Belief can be tentative and conjectural. The evidence of faith is on the same epistemological footing as 'secular' knowledge, and the type of religion engendered by such religious belief is necessarily 'matter of fact', cautious, mildly rationalistic. Though, as was seen in the case of F. R. Tennant, a certain amount of emphasis is put on faith as 'venture', this is not, according to him, a peculiar feature of religion but is something that it has in common with other rational disciplines e.g. natural science. All rational disciplines require the 'faith principle' to venture where they cannot see.

In the case of John Hick's model of religious faith there are two different strands to consider : his remarks about faith as knowledge, and about 'eschatological verification'. He believes that faith in God has particular consequences, but the grounds for this belief are not an examination of nature, or acceptance of a revelation, but a direct experience of God. There is nothing here and now that would conclusively falsify or verify the claims made by the believer, on Hick's model, because (and Hick stresses this) God reveals himself to men through ambiguous evidence, which can be and is 'taken' in different ways by different people. The God who reveals himself is *deus absconditus*. So that any evidence that is appealed to for the verification of God's existence, or for his having a particular character, or for the non-existence of God, is ambiguous. Further, the evidence is not 'all in'. Hick stresses that the believer is an epistemological pilgrim, and that on the basis of partial and incomplete evidence, which the believer chooses to see in a particular way, to give a particular interpretation to, he believes that certain things will happen in the future.[9]

The distinctive point about this view is that its source is not in revelation regarded as a public body of writings from God, but in revelation as the immediate experience by individuals of God, of experiencing the world as mediating the divine presence, and so on. It is not at all clear how, on the basis of such experiences alone (remembering that such documents as the Bible are

[9] This is the basis of Hick's theodicy in *Evil and the God of Love.*

on this view simply records of past encounters), the believer is able to make predictions about the future : that is, how experiences not in themselves unambiguous (that do not involve propositions whose meaning is clear, and that do not involve propositions at all), can yield such propositions as 'God will do x at the end of time' is not clear. How is it possible to guard against reading into such experiences of God what one wants to get out of them? The religious character of this faith is highly individualistic, yielding an optimistic faith that cannot be rebutted by present evidence to the contrary.

The matter is even more complicated in the case of religious belief as certainty grounded in the self-authenticating character of a document. For one thing, it is possible that in such testimony there is a great diversity (logically speaking) of propositions – about God, about history, about what the religious believer's attitude to the world is to be, about the future and so on. To go into each of these now would take us too far afield, and in any case some of the remarks that follow later in the chapter will be relevant. But in general it can be said, about those sentences that purport to say something about the character and doings of God, that they have what Heimbeck has called 'entailments and incompatibles'.[10] Given that God, according to the revelation, has such and such a character, such and such purposes etc., then this will entail that certain things will happen and be incompatible with the happening of other things.

II

We saw earlier that another way of taking the Flew challenge is as 'What reasons would induce A to change his mind as to p?' If this is posed to the various models of belief we have sketched, there are some interesting similarities to and differences from the answers to the first challenge about falsification. For Kantian regulative faith (as far as can be judged from what Kant says) nothing would make A change his mind except a renunciation of the *summum bonum* as a goal, and this would involve the renunciation, according to Kant, of his moral agency. Because for Kant the existence of God is not a cognitive matter, the

[10] *Theology and Meaning*, ch. 5.

question of his existence and of the belief of men in his existence are not two separable questions. 'God exists but is not believed in by anyone' is a contradiction for Kant. Where there is no morality there is no God, for without morality there is no pure practical reason, and without pure practical reason there can be no postulates of the pure practical reason.

For Kant there is no place for the idea of 'loss of religious belief'. Despite certain formal similarities between Wittgenstein's view of religion and that of Kant, Wittgenstein certainly has a place for this phenomenon, at least as interpreted by D. Z. Phillips. *Prima facie* it would seem that if no evidence could count for belief, and none against, then no place could be found for loss of belief. But loss of belief does occur. (It is this fact that loss of belief does occur, rather than the theoretical question of how the notion of loss of belief can be fitted into Wittgenstein's ideas about religion, that prompts Phillips's account.) What he says stems from the idea, discussed earlier, that religious doctrines such as the Last Judgement function as focal points of attention and of moral endeavour for the believer, as pictures, though not literal pictures, which exert a 'hold' over the mind of the believer. Phillips suggests that when loss of belief occurs

'the *attention* of the individual has been won over either by a rival secular picture, or, of course, by worldliness etc. Because his energies are now focused in another direction, this picture which was once powerful in his life, has lost its grip.'[11]

The way Phillips puts this is significant. The believer does not change his mind as (say) his estimation of the evidence changes. Rather, 'his attention is won over'. That is to say, the question 'What would make you change your mind as to p?' is wrongly or badly posed, for what is involved in religious belief is something that is primarily affective, not cognitive. The point to stress here is that *qua religious* beliefs such beliefs are unshakeable. It is their being unshakeable that gives them their character *as* religious beliefs. To the extent that they are abandoned (*not* refuted) to that extent the believer becomes an unbeliever. As with Kant (whatever the other differences), the model of belief

[11] 'Belief and Loss of Belief – A Discussion', *Sophia* (April 1970), p. 4.

consisting of the entertaining and considering of propositions, and then their acceptance or rejection on certain grounds, is quite foreign to Wittgenstein. But unlike Kant, because religion, though connected with morality, is not a necessary postulate of morality, it is possible to conceive of loss of belief. This idea of loss of belief is consistent with the 'pluralism' of this account of religion, of religion as one form of life among many others, including ethics.

Just as evidence counts against the truth of religious propositions for the Locke-Butler model, so it counts against their credibility. Because belief is to be proportioned to evidence, to query the evidence is to question the belief. The evidence that would tend to falsify the proposition that the bomb attack was the work of Spanish dissidents is the same evidence that would tend to make rational people disbelieve that the attack was their work. As the evidence increases/decreases so it becomes increasingly/decreasingly rational to believe p. There is nothing that makes a belief a religious belief – certainly not a peculiar epistemological structure – except that it is concerned with a particular range of matters called 'religious'.

This point can be put in terms of what W. K. Clifford called the 'ethics of belief',[12] as follows. For Locke and Butler 'A has adequate evidence for p, a particular religious proposition' entails 'p is probably true', and 'p ought to be believed'. The ethics of belief for religious propositions are exactly the same as for any set of empirical propositions. For Calvin and Owen, by contrast, 'A has adequate evidence for p, a religious proposition' entails 'p is revealed by God', and 'A ought to believe p'. Each of these two positions applies different criteria of belief.

Yet both the Calvin-Owen and the Locke-Butler views are to be contrasted with, say, the position of Kierkegaard. Both say that religious propositions ought to be believed because of the evidence for them. For Calvin-Owen the evidence is the proposition's *revealedness*; for Butler it is its *probability*. The contrast

[12] On this point see W. K. Clifford, 'The Ethics of Belief' in *Lectures and Essays* II, pp. 163–205; also Roderick Firth, 'Chisholm and the Ethics of Belief', *Philosophical Review* (1959), p. 493. It might be argued that Butler could contrast the present probability of faith with the future certainty of sight. But such a contrast is not open to him because for him it is only probable that there will be life after death.

noted in Owen between faith and sight is not the contrast between faith and reason that Kierkegaard makes but between the evidence provided by the senses and the evidence provided by God in his word.

It is possible that the failure to separate clearly the questions (c) 'What would falsify p?' and (d) 'What reasons would induce A to change his mind as to p?' in the Flew challenge, is due to the fact that the answer to both questions would be the same for Flew and for anyone taking a broadly Locke-Butler view of religious belief – a view which has been so influential with religious believers (and unbelievers) with a strong bias to empiricism. It is worth underlining that the questions are different.

This difference can be shown in terms of Hick's account. The first question, as has been seen, Hick answers in terms of the notion of eschatological verification. The second is answered in terms of the quality of the experience of God, or the experience that is taken to be an experience of God. Hick says little about this, and what features it possesses. What he does say shows that he takes the two questions separately, but his answers to them raise difficulties over the consistency of his account.

It was noticed in the last chapter that Hick stresses what he calls the 'cognitive freedom' of faith. This requires that faith is free in the sense of uncompelled, and therefore that the evidence for faith is ambiguous. The thrust of Hick's remarks is on faith as voluntarily choosing to see or interpret certain experiences as mediating the divine presence. In discussing the question of the rational certainty of the existence of God he says :

'It seems that a sufficiently vivid religious experience would entitle a man to claim to know that God is real. Indeed if his sense of the divine presence is sufficiently powerful he can hardly fail to make this claim. He is sure that God exists, and in his own experience of the presence of God he has a good, and compelling, reason to be sure of it.'[13]

This suggests that a person can experience God so vividly (or, rather, have such a vivid experience) as to be sure of the existence of God, and this suggests that unbelief for such people would be

[13] *Faith and Knowledge*, p. 210.

impossible. They have a compelling reason to be sure of the existence of God. On the other hand, there are certain difficulties with this. For one thing, because Hick's account of faith is heavily voluntaristic, one can choose not to have faith. So that unbelief is always open. If this is so, the use of 'compelling' in the paragraph quoted above is misleading, and inconsistent with the rest of the account. It may be that Hick wants to distinguish between a compelling experience and an experience that compels the belief that p. But this distinction would be hard to make out, and would still be inconsistent with the idea of faith as uncompelled choosing to see-as, or experience-as.

So, roughly, Hick would say that Jones will change his mind as to p if he has certain experiences, or fails to have them, as the case may be. But this failure to believe would not alter the truth-conditions of the proposition believed, for the truth-conditions of 'God exists' are not conditions of human experience. So that 'No one experiences x as mediating the divine presence, but God exists' is not a self-contradiction.

In the case of faith as certainty grounded in self-authenticating testimony the matter is more complicated. Here it is possible only to make a few suggestions, sufficient to underline the differences and similarities between this and the other models of religious belief discussed. Earlier it was shown that the certainty is, logically, an intuition, the believer taking the revelation to be a self-authenticating document as a message of forgiveness and reconciliation. It has a peculiar aptness because of certain needs that the believer regards himself as having, a particular 'power' as John Owen called it. Being in this condition is a necessary condition of being certain that the Bible is the revelation of God. The revelation authenticates itself to those who ask certain questions of it, arising out of their needs. If they were no longer to ask those questions, then the revelation would no longer be regarded as formerly. That is, what matters for belief is relevance.

Much biblical language is that of invitation, of invitations to trust, to prove, to 'taste and see'. These are not invitations to experiment with God as one might with a lump of salt; rather they are invitations to enter into relationship with God. The 'experimental situation' of such a relationship is not public in the sense that it is quite independent of the general psychological states and responses of people, as lumps of salt and experiments on them are independent, nor in the sense that they can be checked independently of the state of the experimenter, as *par excellence*, scientific statements can be checked. Thus if the invitations or promises of the revelation are for some reason regarded as irrelevant they will have no 'power' and not be self-authenticating as God's revelation.

In certain respects this account bears a similarity to the remarks of Phillips discussed earlier, except that relevance is construed as not exclusive of teleological considerations. But the ideas of the object of faith being a *gestalt*, a 'picture', and a believer as one who has been 'captured' by a particular picture, are common elements.

Because, on this account, belief arises as a result of certain intuitions, it is possible to maintain the contrast between faith and sight. Belief can be understood as trusting in what the believer regards as God's promises, despite present appearances. For instance, the story of Abraham is only intelligible on such an account of belief, for the point about Abraham is that he took God to have made promises and that he did not abandon his belief in these promises when the evidence went the other way. He did *not* proportion his belief to the evidence.

What this means is that in asking the question 'What would have to happen for you to abandon belief in God and what he has said?', some attention has to be given, in the case of belief as assent to testimony, to the meaning of what the believer takes God to have said, or promised. It is not simply the case, on this model, that God has told men certain things that they would not otherwise know (Locke's view of revelation), but that he has made certain promises, issued certain warnings, and so forth. The 'logic of believing' in these circumstances will be very different from the logic of believing in certain empirical hypotheses, and judged by such standards it will often appear irrational.

III

For some accounts of religious belief the two questions, 'What is it to believe in God?' and 'Why is it that many people do not believe in God?' are really one question. Yet for both the view of religious belief as a probability-judgement and as belief in self-authenticating divine testimony, the two questions are separate. On the probability view, to believe is to give assent to certain propositions, and the question of the meaningfulness or otherwise of religious propositions only arises as (rather misleadingly) the question of evidence. The same theory of meaning is operative in the case of religious and non-religious, factual, contingent propositions, and so the answer to the second question can only be that there is not regarded as being enough evidence for the truth of certain religious assertions. Inability to find religion meaningful can only be due to refusal to face the evidence of nature or 'scripture history', and to regard them as probably true propositions.

Hick must regard the two questions as two aspects of the same question, because a certain sort of choice is a necessary and sufficient condition both for faith (understood on the model of 'cognition-in-presence') and for the intelligibility of religion. To believe is to choose to see a certain significance in the events and states of one's environment. Hick says little or nothing about what prompts such choice except to stress its freedom, and (as was mentioned earlier) by this he seems to mean, at least in his theodicy in *Evil and the God of Love*, something close to contra-causal freedom, or at least a freedom that is incompatible with divine foreknowledge, and certainly incompatible with divine fore-ordination. Those people who find religion meaningless are just those who have not chosen to attach certain significance to their experience, to see it as mediating the divine presence.

If these two questions are in effect one question, this fact raises certain problems about unbelief, or the absence of religious cognition, and about how Hick is to account for this, theoretically, in terms of his account. Normally if A believes p, and B believes not-p, this entails that p has the same meaning for both A and B. But for Hick this cannot be. To put this in his idiom, in terms of perception, believer and unbeliever do not see the same things (or if they see the same things, they do not interpret them in the same ways, or attach the same significance to them). So that faith does not seem to be the polar opposite of un-faith.

There are at least three possible responses to this difficulty. First, to accept it. Un-faith would then be not simply blindness, but a case of living in a different, and (from the believer's standpoint) poorer world.

A second response is to argue in the same way as D. Z. Phillips. Initially, Phillips is in the same position as Hick on this issue, for both of them want to say that to discover that there is a God is to discover that there is a universe of discourse that the believer had been previously unaware of.[14] Like Hick, Phillips wishes to say that with respect to the existence of God there cannot be detachment and neutrality. That is, for Phillips there is a necessary connection between belief in the existence of God and a whole range of conative and affective responses – worship, trust (or distrust), obedience (or rebellion), and so forth, just as for Hick there is a necessary connection between faith and acknowledgement of the existence of God. (This is not to say that the theses of the two are identical, but that there are analogies at this point.)

So *prima facie* Phillips has the same problem as Hick, the problem of how unbelief is possible. His argument is that belief in God is distinct from trust in God, and that belief in God is compatible with fear. Hick could adopt a position like this, but he says nothing about giving an account of unbelief, and what he says about the voluntary character of the recognition in which faith consists would seem to take him in a different direction from Phillips, who is quite 'Augustinian' on this point.[15]

The third possibility is to argue like S. C. Brown, who takes the position, similar to Hick, that religious belief is a matter of 'insight' – coming to understand p and seeing p as true are indistinguishable. Whereas the dichotomy between understanding a claim and recognizing it as true applies to matter-of-fact claims, it does not apply to what Brown calls grammatical claims. His solution is to argue that 'Even though he (the rejector of Christian

---

[14] D. Z. Phillips ed. *Religion and Understanding*, p. 67.
[15] ibid., p. 78.

belief) may not know what it is for such beliefs to be true, this does not preclude him from finding them sufficiently intelligible to know what it would be for them to be false.'[16] Brown argues that it is possible to reject as false a thesis that is unintelligible in the sense that it is not known what it would be for it to be true, and because it is incompatible with what he holds to be true. Yet it is hard to see how anyone can be in a position to know that a proposition p is incompatible with other propositions q, r and s that are known to be true, if it is not known what p means.

It is not the purpose of this section to argue which of these solutions, if any, is open to Hick, but only to note that because of the way in which 'believing' and 'finding intelligible' are assimilated there is a *prima facie* difficulty.

Finally, it is necessary to consider belief as belief in a self-authenticating revelation. For this model of religious belief the two questions are distinct, for religious belief is understood as involving assent of a certain kind (though it is not perhaps exhaustible in terms of assent). So that to believe is (at least) to assent to certain sentences taken to be the speech of God. The individual believer believes when he takes the speech-acts to be belief-worthy, and belief-worthiness is a function both of the meaning of the propositions, and their meaningfulness or point.

The meaning of the proposition is the same for both believer and unbeliever. This must be so because of the insistence of Owen on what he calls a natural knowledge of supernatural things. That is, it is possible to believe p for the wrong reasons, and so the distinction between believer and unbeliever cannot lie in the fact that one finds a certain utterance meaningful, the other meaningless. As Owen puts it, the distinction between believer and unbeliever is in the 'power', not in what is believed.[17] The proposition is the same for both. So that 'discerning the excellency of p' is part of the meaning of '(truly) believing p', but the excellency of p is not part of the meaning of p if by meaning is meant the sense and reference of the terms.

A reminder about the distinction between 'meaning' and 'meaningfulness' made in the first chapter. To say that a sentence is meaningless may mean either that one or more of its crucial terms

[16] *Do Religious Claims Make Sense?*, p. 143.
[17] *Works*, ed. Goold, IV, pp. 56, 60.

lacks a sense, or that the sentence as a whole is meaningless because it is either syntactically ill-formed or flouts some category-
rule or fails to pass some philosophical criterion of meaning. It
is possible for someone to argue that religious propositions have
meaning in all these senses, and he may be able to show this by
giving the propositions concerned a rough paraphrase. Yet in a
further sense of 'meaning' they may still be meaningless to him,
in that he does not see the point or function of the proposition
concerned, and this may be because he is not aware of any needs
that the proposition is designed to fulfil. He may see that a particular form of words is a command from 'God' but not a command from God, say.

It is clear how someone who took roughly this position would
respond to MacIntyre's point :

'Yet sceptic and believer disagree *in toto* in their judgements on
some religious matters; or so it seems. So how can they be in
possession of the same concepts? If I am prepared to say *nothing*
of what you will say about God or sin or salvation, how can my
concepts of God, sin and salvation be the same as yours? And
if they are not, how can we understand each other?'[18]

There are two points about this. The first is that there are various
sorts of disagreement that can be envisaged. One can agree with
another person on the meaning of 'fairy' but disagree on whether
there are fairies. In the same way sceptics and believers can talk
about God, and disagree on whether he exists or not, and they
can talk about him because both accept certain definitions. And
so, and this is the second point, when MacIntyre claims, in the
above quotation, that there can be a situation in which one
party in a dispute is 'prepared to say *nothing*' that the other is
prepared to say, this is woefully ambiguous. He may mean *say*,
or he may mean *assert*. It may be true of the sceptic and the
believer that they are not able to *assert* the same things of God
simply because one believes in him and the other does not. But
this does not mean that they are not able to speak about 'God'.
It is not that they both believe in his existence but can agree on
nothing about him, nor that neither can agree even on a set of

[18] 'Is Understanding Religion Compatible with Believing?', in *Faith and
the Philosophers*, ed. J. Hick, p. 115.

definitions, but that they cannot make the same assertions. But this does not imply anything about the concepts of 'God or sin or salvation' that each of the parties is using. MacIntyre's confusion is based on a failure to distinguish between the meaning of a proposition and its meaningfulness.

So that, in terms of the discussion of a couple of paragraphs earlier, the sceptic may agree with the believer on a set of definitions, and a set of hypothetical propositions ('If God exists he must be omniscient') and so can be said, in MacIntyre's phrase, to agree on some judgements employing the concepts, while disagreeing totally about the truth of a certain set of religious assertions. The difference between belief and unbelief is not simply a matter of disagreeing on definitions, but can occur, and perhaps typically does occur, when terms are agreed on.

Even where it is possible to agree on the sense and reference of the terms of religious propositions, to allow that there are no philosophical objections to the meaning of religious claims, and to allow that such claims are meaningful (that they have a point or function), this is not sufficient for religious *trust* even though it is sufficient for religious *belief*. It is at this point – where a man understands but does not trust – that the notion of religious rebellion fits into this model of religious belief.

The difference between believing on rational, 'natural' grounds and believing supernaturally is that the propositions that are believed supernaturally are regarded by the believer as certain. The grounds for his belief are internal to the proposition or speech-act concerned. This does not mean that the external grounds are altogether useless, but though they have an apologetic value (to rebut certain objections) they do not provide the grounds for true religious belief. It is because religious propositions become more believable, not more rationally founded, that they are believed. Their credibility is due to their meaning; their being believed consists in the capacity they have for identifying and satisfying needs in the life of the believer. This power is intrinsic to the meaning of the words in the sense that the meaning is a necessary condition of the needs being identified and raised. But the power to identify and raise these needs is not part of what the words mean, because, as was indicated earlier, propositions can be understood and believed for the wrong reasons, and disbelieved as well. The power of the propositions, their capacity to raise and satisfy needs, is both a function of the meaning of the propositions and the disposition of the believer. This is what Owen seems to be saying, and it is clearly linked with what he says elsewhere about self-authentication, which was discussed in Chapter 6. To say 'God exists, but I could not care less' may show that the speaker does not understand what it means to believe in God, but it does not show that he does not understand what the proposition 'God exists' means.

If this account of the religious belief as assent to self-authenticating divine testimony view is right, then the reason for believing p is found in the character of the proposer of p, God who cannot lie, as well as the believer's own needs, the questions he asks arising out of these needs and so forth. This affects the creditworthiness of the proposition, and its relevance, but not its meaning, in the sense of sense and reference. Owen is certainly not saying that the grounds for faith lie in the intuition itself.

There is of course a sense in which there can be a difference of meaning, in the sense of sense and reference, involved. This is the point about the distinction, frequently made, between 'facts' and 'interpretation', which was briefly discussed in the last chapter when dealing with various sorts of scepticism in religion. One kind of scepticism, as we saw, is that people may accept that an event happened but not accept a particular interpretation of it, not accept that it has the significance that others give it. We saw that Hick wishes to interpret this distinction in terms of 'seeing as'. How would someone like Owen interpret it? Part of what he would mean is that two people differ in the interpretation of an event that they agree took place, because they differ about some of the truth-conditions of the proposition describing the event. Take 'Jesus Christ was crucified'. One necessary truth-condition of this proposition is that a certain individual died. Provided that people can agree on an identifying description of 'Jesus Christ' and agree that a person fitting this description died at such a time and place, then they can agree on the fact that Jesus Christ was crucified. But they will differ about the significance of this fact if, for example, they differ about other features of the individual 'Jesus Christ', one believing him to be the divine Messiah, another a lunatic. One way of interpreting the conversion of Saul of Tarsus would be to say that, as a result of his experiences on the road to Damascus, he came to accept that propositions about Jesus were not propositions about a heterodox Jew but about the Messiah, and that certain of the propositions about the Messiah, such as that he died and rose again, were true.

To the further question, that bothers so many theologians and religious people at present, why it is that people do not find religious language meaningful, when by this is meant 'don't find it relevant', Owen's reply would be that they do not discern the kind of relevance concerned, or that they do not accept the need for that kind of relevance. This failure might well be expressed in perceptual terms – such people are 'blind', they do not 'see the light'. Owen, as well as the Bible, uses this kind of language repeatedly. But the answer to the question of what it is to have faith in God cannot be put in such terms, because of the propositional character of religious belief on this view, and because such propositions have a 'public' meaning, a meaning discernible to all.

There is a final case, already mentioned in the case of Phillips and Malcolm. For Owen, as for these philosophers, religious belief has typically a pro-affective element; the believer, typically, trusts the one whose propositions he believes, not simply in the sense that he takes them as reliable, but that he actively relies on the one whose propositions they are. It is thus possible to conceive of someone who assents to p for the right reasons, but who does not trust, and who is frightened of the one believed. Owen would agree with Malcolm that 'Belief in God will involve some affective state or attitude, having God as its object, and those attitudes could vary from reverential love to rebellious rejection'.[19] There are thus three kinds of disbelief to be fitted into this last account of religious belief – belief for the wrong reasons, disbelief due to a complete failure to understand the meaning (i.e. sense and reference) of religious language, and distrust.

[19] Quoted by Phillips, *Faith, Scepticism and Religious Understanding*, p. 78.

INDEX